THE
Mystery Readers' Advisory

The Librarian's Clues
TO
Murder AND Mayhem

ALA READERS' ADVISORY SERIES

The Mystery Readers' Advisory
The Librarian's Clues
to Murder and Mayhem

John Charles ■ Joanna Morrison
Candace Clark

AMERICAN LIBRARY ASSOCIATION
Chicago and London
2002

While extensive effort has gone into ensuring the reliability of information appearing in this book, the publisher makes no warranty, express or implied, on the accuracy or reliability of the information, and does not assume and hereby disclaims any liability to any person for any loss or damage caused by errors or omissions in this publication.

Project editor, Eloise L. Kinney

Cover and text design by Dianne M. Rooney

Composition by Angela Gwizdala in OldStyle 7 and Friz Quadrata using QuarkXpress 4.11 on a PC platform

Printed on 50-pound white offset, a pH-neutral stock, and bound in 10-point cover stock by McNaughton & Gunn

The paper used in this publication meets the minimum requirements of American National Standard for Information Sciences—Permanence of Paper for Printed Library Materials, ANSI Z39.48-1992. ∞

Library of Congress Cataloging-in-Publication Data

Charles, John, 1962-
    The mystery readers' advisory : the librarian's clues to murder and mayhem / John Charles, Joanna Morrison, and Candace Clark.
        p.   cm. — (ALA readers' advisory series)
    Includes bibliographical references and index.
    ISBN 0-8389-0811-X
    1. Fiction in libraries—United States. 2. Libraries—United States—Special collections—Detective and mystery stories. 3. Readers' advisory services—United States. 4. Detective and mystery stories—Bibliography. I. Morrison, Joanna. II. Clark, Candace, 1950- III. Title. IV. Series.

Z711.5 .C48 2002
025.2'78088372—dc21   2001045083

Printed in the United States of America

06   05   04   03   02   5   4   3   2   1

CONTENTS

ACKNOWLEDGMENTS

The authors of this book would like to thank the following individuals for their invaluable contributions, thoughtful criticisms, and support of this project: Joanne Hamilton-Selway, Shelley Mosley, Pam Billard, Natalie Abbott, Kristin Ramsdell, Ann Bouricius, Ben Abeyta, Jennifer Saunders, Dorothy Pulkrabek, Carolyn Butler, Anna Quan Leon, Jeanette Frantz, Becky Henry, Lois Whelan, Bill Pillow, Sharon Laser, and Skye Winter. Joanna would like to acknowledge the contributions made by her parents, Rodney H. Morrison and Betty Jean Morrison, who not only taught her to read (especially mysteries, thank you, Mama!), but that reading is as necessary, natural, and normal as breathing. Candace thanks Mom and Dad for encouraging her to "keep her nose stuck in a book" and thanks the children and future mystery readers of Scottsdale for twenty-five great years. John would like to thank Boo, Oreo, and Blackberry, all of whom helped in their own way.

The authors would also like to thank the staff of ALA Editions, including Marlene Chamberlain, Mary Huchting, Dianne M. Rooney, Janet Russell, and most especially Eloise L. Kinney, for their hard work on this book.

INTRODUCTION

It doesn't take Sherlock Holmes to deduce that mysteries are popular with readers. In 2000, mystery/detective/suspense fiction comprised 28.1 percent of all popular fiction sales in North America (Romance Writers of America). The mystery genre claims an equal, if not greater, share of best-seller lists around the country. The number of independent bookstores devoted to mystery and crime fiction has mushroomed from the very first bookstore dedicated to mysteries, which opened in 1972, to the more than fifty mystery bookstores scattered across the country today. *Library Journal* reports that "mystery reigns as genre king," commanding the highest percentage of adult book expenditures for genre fiction in 1997 by the libraries surveyed (Hoffert 1998, 109). Even the number of patrons in our libraries who ask us "Where are your mysteries?" underscores how popular this type of fiction is with readers.

The purpose of this book is to provide library staff with an introduction to the mystery genre as well as offer tips and techniques for providing mystery readers' advisory services in your library. This book was not intended to be a comprehensive bibliography of the mystery genre. There are other reference sources better suited to this task (some of which are included in our section on reference sources). We have included some of our own bibliographies with a selection of renowned and favorite titles partly to help those of you new to the mystery genre, but also because, as librarians, we just can't seem to help compiling lists. However, these book lists are just a sampling of the riches that await the mystery reader.

In the same manner, we have included a short history of the mystery genre, because knowing the roots of a genre can help the novice readers' advisor put authors and titles into place. This section, however, was not intended to be the definitive history of mysteries. In addition, although we have tried to use as many examples of mystery authors and titles as we could throughout this book, there are other mystery authors and titles that we were not able to mention that could prove to be equally popular with your readers.

One of the things that quickly became the most apparent to us as we wrote this book is that defining a fiction genre, as well as deciding how to subdivide it, is tricky and exhausting work. One person's cozy mystery is another person's soft-boiled mystery. Some readers include romantic suspense in the mystery genre; others insist this type of book belongs in the romance genre. Our divisions of the mystery genre are just that— ours. If another arrangement works better for your readers, feel free to use it. Readers' advisory work is part science and part art, and, like any other artist, you will need to adapt your tools and your materials to your own environment.

Although readers' advisory work is filled with potential perils as well as the opportunity for pratfalls, there is no denying the immense satisfaction that comes from having a reader come back and tell us how much he or she enjoyed a book we suggested. Reprinting book lists because you cannot keep enough in stock or refilling displays that look like reading locusts have gone through them somehow makes all the work that goes into these things worthwhile. The glow you get after a well-received program or book discussion group meeting goes a long way toward repaying the time and effort that were invested in such an event. These are just a few of the rewards we receive when we take the time to provide readers' advisory services to our patrons.

So, as we begin our journey into the world of mystery, crime, and suspense, let us hearken to the words of that immortal detective Sherlock Holmes: "Come, Watson, come! The game is afoot."

1

Mysteries:
Why Readers Love Them

Mysteries offer readers a world where justice and order prevail. They are a modern version of the medieval morality play, in which good and evil battle for dominance. All too often in the real world, justice is not served, order is not restored, and the guilty are not punished. How very satisfying, then, for many readers to see the reverse come true with mysteries. In mystery fiction, actions do have consequences. The underlying sense that justice, in some form or another, will prevail is a powerful reason why readers are drawn to mysteries.

The innate structure of mysteries themselves is another factor that draws some readers to the genre. In mystery fiction, as is the case with most other genre fiction, books have a beginning, a middle, and an end. A crime is committed, an investigation is pursued, a guilty party is denounced. This orderly plot structure can exert a strong appeal to readers who have no taste for some types of contemporary fiction in which nothing is ever resolved and the reader is not even sure what has happened.

Yet another reason why readers are drawn to mysteries is the puzzle aspect of their plots. For some readers there is nothing like the challenge of trying to solve the crime before the author's detective reveals everything.

The attraction of the puzzle has always been an important part of the mystery genre. Some of the most influential writers early in the mystery genre's history have been puzzle crafters. This type of mystery reached its pinnacle of popularity in the genre's first golden age, between the 1920s and 1940s.

Agatha Christie built her reputation as a fiendishly clever mystery plotter, and she spun an amazing number of mystery plots in which the killer ranged from the least likely to the most likely suspect. Golden age mystery writer John Dickson Carr become known as the king of the "locked room" mystery for his ability to craft mysteries in which seemingly impossible crimes were committed. Ellery Queen challenged readers with the question "Do you know who did it?" One thing all of these puzzle-centered mysteries have in common is that they must "play fair" with readers. Nowhere is the importance of the puzzle aspect of mystery reading more apparent than the contretemps that arose with the publication of Christie's *The Murder of Roger Ackroyd*. Some readers claimed the author did not play fair with her plot, and others insisted that the "Queen of Crime" gave them everything they needed to solve this murder. Matching wits with the genre's most celebrated sleuths has been and will continue to be a major reason for the popularity of mysteries.

It is tempting to theorize that the puzzle aspect of mysteries is one reason why the genre is so popular with librarians. Many of us are drawn to the library profession because of the appeal of searching out answers to reference questions and helping patrons locate information on a variety of topics. As readers we can experience this same thrill of searching and hunting for information, though in this case for clues and the identity of the murderer, when we read mysteries.

The pleasure of solving a puzzle-driven mystery is certainly one reason readers are drawn to this genre, but there are plenty of others. Some readers are attracted to mysteries for the characters. Whether it is Sue Grafton's Kinsey Millhone, Susan Wittig Albert's China Bayles, or Rita Mae Brown's Mary Minor Haristeen and her cat, Mrs. Murphy, some readers just want to spend time with these characters. This goes a long way in explaining the appeal of the mystery series because it allows the reader to get to know the sleuths through several volumes and to watch the changes that go on in their lives. For some mystery readers, these characters become as real to them as their neighbors or friends. The attachment of readers to their favorite sleuth is nothing new. Perhaps the most celebrated example of this occurred when Sir Arthur Conan Doyle attempted to "kill off" Sherlock Holmes, but the public's outrage forced him to bring back the popular detective.

Setting is not always a primary reason why readers might choose a mystery, but it can be an incentive for selecting a particular book. There are mystery writers who are known for their use of locale or setting. The Appalachian backdrop of Sharyn McCrumb's Ballad mysteries is as important to the plot as any of its characters, and the beauty with which McCrumb details this setting is truly magnificent. By using a park ranger as a sleuth, mystery writer Nevada Barr can explore the unique, individual qualities of many of our national parks. Francine Mathews perfectly captures the quiet splendor of Nantucket in her Merry Folger mystery series. Short of traveling there yourself, there is no better way to experience the glory of Venice than through the mysteries of Donna Leon; and Arthur W. Upfield's Napoleon Bonaparte books are a celebration of the Australian outback. Mysteries like these allow readers to feel like they are out adventuring without ever leaving their own homes.

Most mystery readers also like the fact that they can learn a little something while they are enjoying their favorite genre. Many mysteries provide an easy way to acquire a bit of knowledge on a wide variety of subjects. Jonathan Gash is known for giving readers a few tidbits about the world of art and antiquities in his Lovejoy mysteries. Readers can explore various facets of Japanese culture in Sujata Massey's Rei Shimura mysteries. Virginia Lanier opens up the world of search-and-rescue bloodhounds in her books, and Gini Hartzmark uses a variety of different business settings for her Kate Milholland mysteries.

More so than anything else, the reason for the popularity of mysteries with readers is that they are simply good reads. At a time when some contemporary fiction authors dwell overwhelmingly on writing style at the expense of plot and characterization, mystery writers understand the power of an entertaining story, and their readers know they can turn to these authors for a good time.

MYSTERY MYTHS AND MISPERCEPTIONS

Like many other genres, the mystery genre seems to be surrounded by myths, misconceptions, misunderstandings, and, sometimes, even prejudices.

Those who don't read mysteries may have particular ideas and opinions about readers who enjoy this type of fiction. Here are a few of the well-known and well-worn misconceptions about this genre that readers and readers' advisors may encounter.

All Mysteries Are Alike

Those who do not read mysteries themselves are most frequently the ones to utter this preposterous generalization. Mystery fiction is not alone in being perceived as a vast wasteland of uniformity and blandness. This same statement, with the substitution of another genre (romance, western, science fiction, etc.) for mystery, has erroneously been applied by those who wish to dismiss any type of book they have never read themselves. The mistake is often made that simply because genre fiction follows certain structural patterns, the books themselves are formulaic. It is true that in the mystery genre the focus in most books is on solving a crime, but that does not mean that each mystery is alike. The mystery genre is comprised of a number of different subgenres, each with its own unique characteristics. In some cases, such as the suspense and thriller subgenres, the focus of the book may not be on solving a crime, but rather on the protagonist escaping from danger. In addition, authors bring their own unique voices and writing styles to their books. The truth is that there are as many different kinds of mysteries as there are mystery authors.

All Mysteries Must Involve a Murder

Many mysteries do involve the investigation of a murder and search for the killer. The selection of murder as the crime of choice by many authors is simply a reflection that taking another person's life is the ultimate crime. Murder is the most frequently used crime in mystery novels, but there are examples of books in which excellent mysteries are crafted around crimes other than that of murder. Some examples of this type of murderless mystery include Josephine Tey's *The Franchise Affair,* in which it is not a person who is murdered, but rather a reputation. *Aunt Dimity's Death,* by Nancy Atherton, is a classic cozy mystery with no murder. Donald Westlake offers mystery readers several excellent caper books, including *The Hot Rock,* in which murder plays no role in the plot. Dorothy L. Sayers's *Gaudy Night* features her famous sleuths Lord Peter Wimsey and Harriet Vane and focuses on vandalism at an Oxford women's college. Michael Innes's *Money from Holme* is just one example of a mystery that focuses on art theft rather than murder. There are also a number of mystery short stories in which crimes of all kinds, with the exception of murder, are explored.

The Only Reason People Read Mysteries Is to Figure Out Whodunit

Most mysteries do concentrate on the identification of the murderer, but there are mysteries in which guessing the killer is not the primary goal. In "inverted mysteries," as they are sometimes called, the identity of the murderer is known by the reader right from the start. Instead of asking *whodunit,* readers concentrate on *whydunit.* Examples of inverted mysteries include Frances Iles's *Before the Fact,* L. R. Wright's *The Suspect,* and Ruth Rendell's *Judgement in Stone.* In all of these mysteries, the reader immediately knows who the killer is. What they must discover is why the murder was committed.

Another twist on this theme is the classic television show *Columbo.* Each episode opened up with the viewer watching the murderer commit the crime. The viewer knew who did it; the enjoyment came from seeing how police detective Columbo caught the killer.

Some readers choose a particular mystery simply because of an author's voice or writing style. For others, the primary appeal might reside in the book's setting. Still other readers care most about the characters. Discovering the identity of the murderer is just one reason, but not the only reason, that readers enjoy mysteries.

Mysteries Are Merely Escapist Reading

First of all, there is nothing wrong with reading to escape. This is pretty much why readers are drawn to genre fiction in the first place: as a way of escaping the stresses and headaches of ordinary life. But even though the primary goal of many mysteries is simply to entertain readers, mysteries can also offer readers the opportunity to learn something new or explore a serious issue.

Author Abigail Padgett not only crafts compellingly written mysteries, but she also takes on the issues surrounding a detective who suffers from manic-depressive disorder as well as the treatment of abused children in today's world. Contemporary social issues also play a role in a number of other mysteries, and examples could include Nancy Pickard's *Marriage Is Murder,* which delves into the subject of battered wives, or Donald Westlake's *The Ax,* which takes on corporate downsizing.

Mysteries can offer readers the opportunity to discover what it is like to be someone else. Depending on the mystery author, a reader can become an African American domestic worker (Barbara Neely's Blanche White), a gay private eye (Joseph Hansen's Dave Brandsetter), a Navajo FBI agent (Aimee Thurlo and David Thurlo's Ella Clah), a 1920s independent female (K. K. Beck), or a Hollywood party planner and caterer (Jerrilyn Farmer's Madeline Bean).

Mysteries also open up a window into time and give us new insight into the similarities and differences between our lives today and what life was like in the past. Historical mysteries offer a wonderful way to learn a little something about history while at the same time enjoying a great book. For example, reading about Miriam Grace Monfredo's librarian-suffragette-detective Glynis Tryon can give readers a new appreciation and better understanding of the fight for women's rights in this country.

Like any other type of book, mysteries range from light and fun to serious and thought-provoking. For whatever reason a book is chosen, readers should never feel that they must justify their choice of leisure reading.

Most Mystery Writers Pattern Their Detectives after Themselves

Ask some mystery writers about their protagonists, and you will often hear the response, "He or she is just like me, only twelve inches taller and ten pounds lighter." It is true that many mystery writers do draw upon personal experiences when it comes to creating their sleuths. Dashiell Hammett used his own experiences as a detective in creating the "Continental Op." Author Linda Fairstein just happens to share the same job, director of the Sex Crimes Prosecution Unit for the Manhattan District Attorney, as her fictional protagonist, Alexandra Cooper. Dorothy Uhnak relied on her own background as a New York City Transit cop when it came time to give her police detective character, Christine Opara, a realistic flavor. These are just a few examples of mystery authors who pattern their fictional sleuths after their own backgrounds.

However, it is not a requirement that all detectives must be mirror images of their literary parents. For example, author S. J. Rozan's mystery series features detectives Bill Smith, the typical hard-bitten private eye, and Lydia Chin, his younger, American-born Chinese partner. Rozan herself is neither Chinese nor male and by trade is an architect. However, most readers coming to the series without knowing anything about the author might automatically assume that no one who did not share the same background as her characters could write so convincingly and beautifully about them and their world. The truth is that a gifted and talented author can write about any subject and create any protagonist and make the reader care about them.

We could go on and on listing common misperceptions, but you get the gist. Assumptions about mystery fiction, however unconsciously or innocently made, can negatively influence a readers' advisory transaction on both the part of the reader and the librarian. Thus, it behooves the readers' advisor to not only be aware of these "mythperceptions," but to rise above them.

A Short History
of the Mystery

Most experts pinpoint the emergence of the mystery genre in American literature to the mid–nineteenth century, when Edgar Allan Poe published his "tales of ratiocination" and introduced fictional detective C. Auguste Dupin in his 1841 short story, "The Murders in the Rue Morgue." Poe continued Dupin's exploits in works such as "The Mystery of Marie Roget" in 1842 and "The Purloined Letter" in 1845. In these stories, Poe created standard elements of detective fiction—such as the "locked room" mystery and the use of a brilliant, eccentric detective who solves the crime through careful reasoning and examination of devices—that are still being used by mystery writers today.

Poe himself greatly influenced the writings of Charles Dickens, who made his own significant contributions to the literature of the mystery genre, as did Wilkie Collins. Dickens wrote many stories that contained elements of mystery and suspense, including *Bleak House* and *The Mystery of Edwin Drood*. Collins's novels *The Woman in White* and *The Moonstone* are considered by some to be the first true English detective novels.

Male writers did not have a monopoly on the mystery genre, however. English writer Mary Elizabeth Braddon's lurid (for the times) novel *Lady Audley's Secret* featured one of the earliest amateur sleuths. In America, Metta Victoria Fuller Victor, writing under the pseudonym

Seeley Register, is credited with writing the first American detective novel, *The Dead Letter,* which was first serialized and then published in book format in 1867. Register's groundbreaking work in the genre was matched by fellow American Katharine Green, whose 1878 mystery novel, *The Leavenworth Case: A Lawyer's Story,* introduced many now-standard genre conventions, such as the body in the library.

During the late nineteenth and early twentieth centuries, the short story form dominated the mystery genre. Perhaps the most popular writer of mystery short stories in this period was Sir Arthur Conan Doyle, creator of the legendary Sherlock Holmes. With the publication of *A Study in Scarlet* in 1887, readers were introduced to a type of detective that had never been seen before. With his distinctive mannerisms and flair for deducing clues, Holmes and his sidekick Dr. Watson quickly became favorites of mystery readers around the world.

By the end of World War I, the popularity of the mystery short story began to diminish. In the 1920s and 1930s, the novel format became popular again with mystery writers. Authors such as Dorothy Sayers, Mignon G. Eberhart, S. S. Van Dine, and John Dickson Carr gave readers a wide range of detective novels from which to choose. The 1920s ushered in the golden age of mystery fiction for readers and introduced one of the genre's most celebrated authors: Agatha Christie. Christie's first mystery novel, *The Mysterious Affair at Styles,* debuted in 1921, and the world got its first look at detective Hercule Poirot. Christie would go on to earn a place for her mysteries on the best-seller lists for the next five decades, and her work would eventually come to represent the genre to readers worldwide. Christie was joined in the 1920s and 1930s by Great Britain's other "Queens of Crime": Dorothy Sayers, Margery Allingham, and Ngaio Marsh.

The conventions and characteristics of today's cozy mysteries were also born during the first golden age of mystery fiction (Herbert 1999). With their emphasis on a closed circle of suspects, a world of manners and customs, a focus on solving the puzzle by brain rather than by brawn, the use of a number of archetypal characters, and the ultimate goal of restoring order to Mayhem Parva, mysteries by authors such as Christie (whose fictional village of St. Mary's Mead is perhaps the ultimate in cozy villages), Sayers, Allingham, and Marsh set up a pattern that would be followed by their American counterparts, including Mignon G. Eberhart and Ellery Queen as well as cozy mystery writers seventy and eighty years later.

The late 1920s and 1930s also gave rise to two of the most popular juvenile mystery series of the twentieth century: Nancy Drew and the Hardy Boys. Creations of the Stratemeyer Syndicate, the Hardy Boys first appeared in *The Tower Treasure* in 1927, and these two intrepid investigators were soon followed by Nancy Drew, who solved her first case, *The Secret of the Old Clock,* in 1930. A plethora of other resourceful juvenile sleuths would soon follow in the tracks of these perennially popular teen detectives.

American detective fiction reached new heights in the 1930s and 1940s with the immense popularity of the novels of Ellery Queen, a pseudonym used by two American cousins, Manfred B. Lee and Frederic Dannay. Queen's mysteries proved to be so well liked that over the span of forty years the two authors wrote more than thirty-three mysteries featuring the "pure logician." The 1930s also gave rise to the appearance of the "quirky" detective, whose unusual mannerisms or eccentric personalities gave flavor to the stories. One example of this type of sleuth is Earl Derr Bigger's creation, Charlie Chan, who used his Asian wisdom to solve crimes around the Pacific Rim. Another example is Rex Stout's Nero Wolfe, the orchid fancier and gourmand detective who rarely left his New York brownstone home and relied on his partner, Archie Goodwin, for legwork. First appearing in 1933 in *Fer-de-Lance,* Wolfe would solve crimes in thirty-three novels and in more than forty novellas.

At the same time these mannered mysteries were growing in popularity, another type of mystery fiction was entering the scene. Hardboiled novels were born in the 1920s with the rise of popular magazines known as "pulps." *Black Mask,* the most famous of the pulp magazines, started by offering readers adventure stories but eventually began devoting its pages to detective fiction. This magazine with its contributing writers like Dashiell Hammett and Raymond Chandler came to symbolize the hard-boiled school of mystery writing, which strove to reflect the realities of daily life at that time. Detectives such as Hammett's Sam Spade and Chandler's Philip Marlowe were a direct contrast to the more intellectual, sophisticated, and mannered sleuths created by Christie, Van Dine, and Queen. Hard-boiled sleuths were rough, often violent men who lived by their own strict codes of honor. Perhaps the most extreme example of these ultratough sleuths is Mickey Spillane's Mike Hammer, who first appeared in 1947 in *I, the Jury,* which quickly became the best-selling mystery in history up to that time. Spillane's writing took the hard-boiled mystery to the edge, and with its emphasis on sex and violence, it mainly appealed to male mystery readers of that era.

The police procedural mystery rose to prominence in the 1940s and 1950s. Although previous mystery writers may have used a policeman as a sleuth (golden age mystery writer Marsh, for example), these cop sleuths functioned in many ways exactly like their more prevalent amateur sleuth counterparts. Authors such as Lawrence Treat, Hilary Waugh, Dell Shannon, and Ed McBain took a different approach to the policeman as a detective. These authors' mysteries featured cases that brought the reader into the policeman's professional world, showing how these cops, as both individuals and part of a police force, solved crimes.

The 1960s were a decade of change not only for society, but also for the mystery genre. Espionage fiction gained a major share of the mystery market with the popularity of author Ian Fleming's James Bond and his female counterpart, Modesty Blaise, created by Peter O'Donnell. Later in this decade, espionage fiction would see more realistic spy protagonists crafted by John le Carré and Len Deighton. Romantic suspense and gothics written by authors such as Mary Stewart, Phyllis A. Whitney, and Barbara Michaels turned up on the shelves of bookstores and libraries, much to the delight of readers who reveled in these atmospheric blends of danger and romance. This decade also saw two memorable moments for juvenile mysteries: the arrival of Donald J. Sobol's Encyclopedia Brown, who solved his first group of cases in 1963, and the awarding of the first Edgar for a juvenile mystery to Phyllis A. Whitney for her *Mystery of the Haunted Pool,* in 1961.

As the 1960s gave way to the 1970s, mystery fiction continued to reflect the changes going on in society. The private investigator novel once again came to the forefront. Fictional sleuths discovered their sensitive sides, with authors such as Robert B. Parker introducing a softer, more introspective version of the hard-boiled detective. With the publication of *Fadeout,* in 1970, Joseph Hansen offered readers one of the first mysteries to portray a gay private eye in an honest and positive manner. At the same time, women began eyeing the private eye subgenre as fair game for their own literary efforts. P. D. James wrote her first Cordelia Gray mystery, *An Unsuitable Job for a Woman,* in 1972. However, most critics of the private eye subgenre credit Marcia Muller, who wrote her first Sharon McCone mystery, *Edwin of the Iron Shoes,* in 1977, with introducing readers to a new breed of female private detectives. Authors

Sue Grafton and Sara Paretsky, who both published their first female private eye mysteries in 1982, quickly followed Muller.

The 1970s saw the mystery genre gain new depths in terms of the range of choices for readers in both settings and types of sleuths. An excellent example is Tony Hillerman, who took mystery readers to a Navajo reservation with his sleuth Joe Leaphorn in *The Blessing Way,* published in 1970. For many mystery readers, this was their first experience with a mystery series that was not set in one of the traditional big cities, such as New York or Los Angeles. The growing popularity of Hillerman's books demonstrated to publishers that mystery readers could be interested in other cultures and other settings and opened the door for further diversity in terms of locales and types of sleuths.

Going back in time for a setting also became popular in this decade. The historical mystery gained its first real share of the genre with the 1970s. Peter Lovesey opened the decade with *Wobble to Death,* published in 1970, and Elizabeth Peters's first Amelia Peabody mystery, *Crocodile on the Sandbank,* came out in 1975. Ellis Peters's Brother Cadfael historical mysteries got their start with *A Morbid Taste for Bones,* which was published in Great Britain in 1970 and appeared in the United States in 1977. As the decade came to a close, Anne Perry appeared on the scene with her first historical mystery featuring Charlotte and Thomas Pitt, *The Cater Street Hangman.*

The 1980s built on all of these gains as the mystery genre attracted a growing number of readers. Women mystery writers in particular began to play an increasing role in the genre during this decade, and Sisters in Crime, the first mystery organization dedicated to promoting mystery fiction by female authors, was born in 1986. The legal thriller became fashionable again with the publication of Scott Turow's *Presumed Innocent* in 1987. Turow's success would inspire a whole crop of legal-eagle writers, including the subgenre's reigning king, John Grisham.

Though they had been around almost since the mystery genre itself was born, there was a sudden tremendous increase in demand for cozy mysteries in the 1980s. In 1982, Virginia Rich penned her first book, *The Cooking School Murders,* giving many readers their first taste of a cozy culinary mystery. Joan Hess debuted her first Claire Cross mystery, *Strangled Prose,* and Carolyn Hart gave readers bookstore owner sleuth Annie Darling, in *Murder on Demand,* in the 1980s. Other cozy mystery writers who got their start at this time included Alisa Craig, Gillian

Roberts, Martha Grimes, and Valerie Wolzien. Mysteries written in the cozy manner would become so popular that a whole convention, Malice Domestic, celebrating this type of mystery was born in 1989.

The 1990s proved to be the new golden age of the mystery. Independent mystery bookstores sprang up around the country; by 1999, there were more than fifty to help feed readers' appetites for mystery books, and the mystery genre gained a new level of popularity. Strong female sleuths continued to attract readers, and authors such as Sue Henry, Dana Stabenow, Nevada Barr, and Jan Burke all debuted their first mystery during the 1990s. The beginning of the decade also saw the arrival of mystery author Patricia Cornwell. Her first book, *Postmortem,* garnered most of the major mystery awards the year it was published, inspired a new interest in forensic mysteries, and helped to give rise to the author as a celebrity phenomenon. Cornwell's meteoric climb up national best-seller lists reflected the growing trend in which mysteries of all kinds, from Diane Mott Davidson's cozy amateur sleuth series to John Sandford's gritty, edgy suspense novels, achieved places on best-seller lists.

Even as mysteries gained new readers and a wider share of the publishing market, there were a few dark clouds on the horizon. Midlist mystery authors discovered a shrinking market for their work as publishers scrambled to find and promote their next best-selling author. The power of the big chain bookstores to affect a mystery writer's career became apparent when at least a few mystery authors were forced to choose between not writing at all or choosing a new pseudonym in order to start fresh in the industry. With the growing trend toward the merger of major publishing houses and consolidation of publishing lines, new mystery authors saw their chances of cracking the traditional market shrinking. Instead of focusing on how well written and original a particular mystery might be, some publishers now seemed to care more about what type of hook a mystery had or how well it could be marketed.

As the 1990s give way to a new century, the common elements defining the mystery genre continue to be that of change and of the blurring among genres. Part of this change is the growing interest in the crime novel rather than just the mystery. Change continues to come to the publishing industry as new small presses are springing up to fill the gaps left by the consolidation and merger of traditional publishers. Print-on-demand technology offers the tantalizing hope that any mystery no longer need be "out of print." No single subgenre dominates the mystery market today, and readers have more choices than ever before. Sleuths of all types, genders, nationalities, and ages continue to seek the answer to "whodunit?" to the continuing delight and pleasure of readers everywhere.

3

Mystery Subgenres: Characteristics and Appeal

"L abels are for jam; a novel is too subtle a blend for simple tagging."
This quote by mystery author Lesley Grant-Adamson (Moody 1990,
77) perfectly captures the inherent difficulties in dividing books into categories or subgenres. Yet librarians love to sort, categorize, and type
books. It makes things so much easier both for us as readers' advisors
and our patrons: if you like title A, you will like title B; or author C
writes just like author D. Even as we struggle to find the perfect definition of a subgenre or the closest match to a popular author, remember
that books can be complex, infinitely layered things that may defy easy
categorization.

Two of the most important things to remember about mystery readers' advisory work are that *not every mystery is alike* and *readers have
individual preferences and tastes.* Learning the differences between mystery subgenres as well as the delicate (and not so delicate) nuances in
individual mystery authors' writing styles are two of the most valuable
things you can do to become an effective readers' advisor.

A reader who asks for recommendations for a new mystery author
wants you to be familiar with the genre itself. There is no quicker way to
lose a reader than to blithely recommend M. C. Beaton's Hamish
McBeth mysteries to someone who likes Ian Rankin's books. It is true
that both of these authors write mysteries featuring police detectives set
in Scotland, but Beaton's McBeth series is cozier and often humorous in

tone while Rankin's mystery series is tough, gritty, and uses the backdrop of the larger cities in Scotland. The differences between these two authors' writing styles and other characteristics place them miles apart in terms of appeal for some readers. The same would hold true for the librarian who suggests the suspense novels of author A. J. Holt to a reader who loves Mary Higgins Clark's books without checking on the patron's individual comfort level in terms of graphic violence. Just because two authors happen to write suspense novels or mysteries does not mean that they are exactly alike and will appeal equally to all readers.

When it comes to defining the mystery genre as a whole, readers' advisors will find there are almost as many ways to delineate the mystery genre as there are mysteries. As far as drawing the line that separates mysteries from other types of literature, critic and author Julian Symons acknowledges, "The precise placing of the line is a matter of individual taste" (1993, 5). *Publishers Weekly* writer Robert Dahlin received a range of responses when he posed the question "What is a mystery?" to editors and booksellers (1996, 38–39). In Dahlin's article some defined the genre quite narrowly, such as editor Michael Seidman, who sees a mystery as "a puzzle—a game—between author and reader." On the other hand, bookstore owner Jim Huang "defines mysteries very broadly. Readers look for a range of subjects, settings, authors, and themes." Scholar and critic Allen J. Hubin also takes a broad approach by describing the mystery genre as any book "containing crime or the threat of crime as the major plot element" (1994, ix). Embracing a fluid definition of the mystery (i.e., any book where crime, mystery, danger, or suspense permeates the core of the plot) is the best way to meet the wide-ranging needs of the genre's readers.

Although finding one perfect definition for the genre as a whole can be difficult—after all, any type of fiction that encompasses authors from Mary Stewart to Clive Cussler to Agatha Christie is certainly diverse—things do become easier when it comes to classifying its subgenres. As with any other fiction genre, the mystery genre is composed of a number of subgenres, or different types of mysteries. When certain mystery books share one or more common elements, they are often grouped together into a subgenre, or subset, of the mystery genre itself. Subgenres are just a way of breaking down the genre into more manageable pieces.

Author Lawrence Block came up with what is perhaps the cleverest way of separating mysteries into subgenres: "those with cats in them and those without" (1993, 302). Although this method of categorizing would certainly make things easier for us as readers' advisors, most of us do need a few more subgenres. The most common characteristic used to define a mystery subgenre is the type of detective a book uses, such as amateur sleuth, police professional, or private eye. Mysteries set in the past are frequently grouped together as historical mysteries. Suspense novels can be subdivided according to the focus of the book, such as the legal environment or the world of spies and espionage.

Some readers, and even publishers, like to sort out mysteries by theme. If the plot revolves around a certain topic, such as gardening, art, or the theater, or if the book is set in a certain geographic location, this can be used as a way of categorizing mysteries. Themed mysteries do play an important role in the genre, but there are literally hundreds of different themes that could be used to catalog mysteries. Thus, by itself, a theme is not always the most useful way to define a subgenre. The popularity of some themes will vary from reader to reader and from library to library, and trying to compile a complete list of every type of themed mystery would prove overwhelming to even the most dedicated readers' advisor.

Although separating mysteries by every type of theme is not a practical option for most readers' advisory staff, you should still be aware of the popularity of certain themed mysteries. By preparing in advance for this type of request, you can meet the needs of your patrons. Therefore, we have included some of our favorite and most requested mysteries by themes, such as "Ecclesiastical Mysteries," in appendix B, page 154.

Things would be so much easier for readers' advisors if there were one master list of mystery subgenres agreed upon by the various mystery reference sources as well as by the readers themselves. Unfortunately, this master list does not exist, and the number and type of mystery subgenres can vary greatly depending upon who is doing the classifying. Pigeonholing mysteries into different categories is difficult and messy work. Sometimes the books themselves defy categorization and may require placement into two different subgenres. The mystery subgenres listed below are the results of years of mystery reading and readers' advisory work on the part of the authors of this book. They are by no means perfect. Readers' advisory staff are encouraged to use these subgenres as a guide, but if mixing two subgenres or creating new subgenre categories works better for your library and your readers, by all means, feel free to do so.

AMATEUR SLEUTH—IF YOU WANT SOMETHING DONE RIGHT, YOU HAVE TO DO IT YOURSELF

Generally, there are two types of amateur sleuths. There are those amateur detectives who seem to enjoy and have a talent for solving crimes. Agatha Christie's Miss Marple and Jessica Fletcher, from the television show *Murder, She Wrote,* are two examples of this type of amateur sleuth. Then there are those people forced by outside circumstances into solving a crime. Examples of this type of amateur sleuth include the husband of the murder victim who must uncover the identity of the real killer to clear his own name or the amateur detective who takes on investigating a murder to avenge the death of the victim.

The amateur sleuth has played a major role in the mystery genre since Edgar Allen Poe's Chevalier C. Auguste Dupin appeared in print in 1841. Many of the golden age sleuths were amateur detectives, including Agatha Christie's Miss Marple, Dorothy Sayers's Lord Peter Wimsey, Margery Allingham's Albert Campion, and S. S. Van Dine's Philo Vance. Amateur sleuths were not just a favorite of adult mystery readers. For decades, juvenile mystery readers have delighted in the amateur sleuthing efforts of Nancy Drew and the Hardy Boys as well as the Three Investigators and Judy Bolton. Even today, the amateur sleuth stars in a significant share of the mysteries published.

The appeal of the amateur sleuth to many mystery readers is that the detective is so very ordinary. Amateur sleuths lack the skills and training professional investigators have and instead must rely on their own instincts and wits. For many readers, it is easier to relate to this type of detective on a personal level, and that is a great part of the attraction. More readers have experienced life in the suburbs as narrated by Valerie Wolzien's sleuth Susan Henshaw or Jill Churchill's Jane Jeffrey than know what it is like to work in a police department like Ed McBain's 87th Precinct.

The amateur sleuth subgenre does have a few conventions of its own. The murderer usually comes from a closed circle of suspects. In other words, the killer is most likely someone the amateur sleuth knows, whether it is one of his or her relatives, a person he or she works with, or someone from the neighborhood. Even more so than with other types of mysteries, readers must also be willing to suspend their sense of disbelief with amateur sleuths because in real life it is highly unlikely that many amateurs would become involved in a murder investigation. For the most part, amateur sleuth mysteries tend to eschew the gritty, graphic details of the crime that can pop up in other mystery subgenres, such as private detective mysteries or serial killer thrillers.

Amateur detectives have several advantages over their professional and police counterparts. An amateur sleuth can frequently obtain more information from suspects than the police simply because he or she is less intimidating. The amateur detective is often more able to successfully blend into the background of a community and unearth tidbits of gossip that can lead to the killer. Many times, the amateur sleuth has personal connections that the police do not have, and the amateur sleuth does not have to play by the same rules that professional detectives and the police must abide by.

Amateur sleuths also face a few difficulties that other types of detectives do not. For one thing, most amateur sleuths have no real powers or authority to investigate a crime or apprehend a killer. In some cases authors may align their amateur sleuths with a professional counterpart such as a police officer who can help with some of these things. Examples of this type of partnership include Diane Mott Davidson's Goldy Bear mysteries, Nancy Pickard's Jenny Cain series, and Richard Lockridge and Frances Lockridge's classic series featuring the Norths. Writers may also choose a particular occupation for their amateur sleuth that helps overcome this problem. Thus, mystery readers will encounter a number of amateur detectives from the fields of journalism, religion, and academia, because each of these professions may offer more opportunities for the sleuth to pry or allow flexible work schedules that do not get in the way of investigating.

Mystery writers who develop a series featuring an amateur sleuth must also derive some creative ways for introducing murder on a repeated basis into their protagonist's lives lest their sleuths come up with the dreaded Cabot Cove syndrome (i.e., the highly improbable number of residents in Jessica Fletcher's tiny hometown of Cabot Cove who became murder victims). One example of a mystery writer who has found a successful solution to this problem is Carole Berry, who, by giving her fictional sleuth Bonnie Indermill the profession of an office temp, has logically been able to move her character from job to job and introduce new murders into the life of her sleuth without it becoming contrived.

Mystery authors may choose the amateur sleuth as their detective for various reasons, but, more often than not, it allows them to draw upon personal knowledge of a specific field. In turn this amateur sleuth's special knowledge or skills is often the very reason why he or she is able to solve a crime instead of the professionals. For example, mystery writer Aaron Elkins uses his own background in anthropology to bring his forensic anthropologist detective Gideon Oliver to life. Author Lynn Hamilton applies her expertise with art, mythology, and antiquities to create her series detective Lara McClintock, an antiquities dealer who solves mysteries around the globe. Emma Lathen, in reality the pseudonym for economist Mary Jane Latsis and lawyer Martha B. Henissart, utilizes a working knowledge of the business world to give verisimilitude to banker sleuth John Putnam Thatcher. The fields of knowledge and range of expertise exhibited by amateur sleuths are infinite. There truly is a sleuth for almost any reader's interests. *(See* appendix A, page 111, for a book list with some of our favorite amateur sleuths.)

PRIVATE INVESTIGATORS—TRENCH COATS, GATS, AND GIRLS

Completely unique, instantly recognizable, and absolutely distinctive, the private investigator (P.I.) novel has proved to be a popular and durable mystery subgenre. What makes a P.I. novel work? It's the appeal of the underdog, to whom the private investigator is drawn, sometimes against his or her will, to help. It's the attraction of the average Dick or Jane who, in spite of disillusionment and cynicism, is still willing to delve into society's seamy underside to expose the truth. It's the fascination with a paladin, who, in spite of dented armor and bad experiences, is still willing to tilt against the windmills of big business, corruption, graft, and sexual misconduct. It is that tough gal or guy whose search for the truth has an element of a forlorn hope. Raymond Chandler, one of the masters of P.I. fiction, summed it up when he wrote in his essay "The Simple Art of Murder" that "down these mean streets a man must go who is not himself mean, who is neither tarnished nor afraid."

Chandler wrote his essay for the *Atlantic Monthly* magazine in part to answer criticism of his brand of hard-boiled fiction as stupid, violent, and unrealistic (1944, 53). These complaints still continue to be leveled against P.I. fiction. Yet it endures, becoming even more popular into the

1990s, which saw an explosion of investigators of both genders and from all kinds of backgrounds.

The earliest P.I. fiction might have been Sir Arthur Conan Doyle's Sherlock Holmes. Often Holmes is thought of as an amateur detective, especially given his famous disdain for Inspector Lestrade and the official London police force. But Holmes took cases for fees and used his own resources, connections, and, ultimately, his powers of investigation to solve his cases. That makes Holmes very similar to the classic private eye. The popularity of Doyle's detective created a rush of similar stories, most fairly forgettable, until the arrival of pulp magazines, which in turn paved the way to the modern private eye novel.

Pulp magazines (so-called because of the extremely cheap and flimsy paper upon which they were printed) made their first appearance in the late 1800s with *Argosy* but had their heyday in the years between the early 1920s and the late 1950s. They offered short stories for every taste, but private investigators were among the most popular. Even now, the mention of pulp magazines reminds readers of the lurid, garish covers featuring a dame in trouble (or making trouble) and the quintessential gumshoe, complete with gun and trench coat. The hard-boiled private investigator became a staple in pulp stories, many of which were written by authors such as Dashiell Hammett, Raymond Chandler, Erle Stanley Gardner, and John D. MacDonald, all of whom would make their names in detective fiction. Indeed, one of Hammett's most famous tales, *The Maltese Falcon,* was first published in serial form in the pulp *Black Mask* in 1930. Most pulp magazines faded away in the 1950s, victims of both the public's changing tastes and the new entertainment medium of television.

A memorable legacy of the old pulps is the most hard-boiled private dick of them all, Mike Hammer. Hammer's creator, Mickey Spillane, first began by contributing stories to the pulps, then later expanded his stories into novels. His most famous creation is Hammer, a comic-bookishly violent, conservative private detective who is suspicious of women (up to and including his loyal secretary, Velda), left-wing politics, and liberals. He was a perfect hero for America during the time of Joseph McCarthy and the House Un-American Activities Committee. In spite of the thin plots and violent story lines, Hammer was a hit, and Spillane sold millions of copies of his books featuring the P.I. with the short fuse. Many Mike Hammer books are still in print, and Hammer's character has appeared on television and in movies.

Other famous authors of private eye novels include Dashiell Hammett, who used his own background as an investigator for the Pinkerton Agency to lend realism to his fictional operative, the Continental Op, named for his place of employment (the Continental Detective Agency), and to his most famous gumshoe, Sam Spade. Spade is a tough and cynical man who puts himself out for no one, but when, in *The Maltese Falcon,* his partner, Miles Archer, is killed, Spade feels compelled to find the truth behind Archer's death. Hammett creates a picture of a man whose private set of ethics may not coincide with those of society but by which he will unswervingly abide. Raymond Chandler's popular character Philip Marlowe is another hard-boiled private eye with a conscience. Even when they prove unworthy, Marlowe can't help himself: in titles such as *Farewell My Lovely* and *The Big Sleep,* he continues to try to save people in trouble.

As private investigator fiction developed, many authors expanded the social conscience of their characters. Ross MacDonald's Lew Archer, although conforming to the popular "P.I. as loner" perception, took cases that arose out of what used to be known as "troubled" families; the term *dysfunctional family* was unknown in 1949, when *The Moving Target,* the first Archer novel, was published. Robert B. Parker's Spenser further softened the edges of private investigator fiction when he appeared in 1973 in *The Godwulf Manuscript.* Spenser is principled, sensitive, and willing to accept helpful insights from his lover, a sophisticated and educated woman. Multicultural private eyes became much more evident, including George Baxt's gay black detective, Pharoah Love, first seen in 1966 in *A Queer Kind of Death.* In the early 1970s, Roger L. Simon created the former college radical and counterculture hippie, Jewish P.I. Moses Wine *(The Big Fix).*

The 1980s and 1990s ushered in an era that featured investigators of both genders and from every kind of background. With some few exceptions (including Erle Stanley Gardner, who, writing as A. A. Fair, had a female P.I., Bertha Cool, who first appeared in *The Bigger They Come* with sidekick Donald Lam in 1939), females found in hard-boiled fiction were either damsels in distress or femmes fatales. Sue Grafton's Kinsey Millhone, Sara Paretsky's V.I. Warshawski, and Marcia Muller's Sharon McCone are all female private investigators who, beginning in the late 1970s, lent a distinctly different perspective to the mean streets and permanently changed the look of P.I. fiction.

British author P. D. James is often credited with creating the first contemporary female private investigator in 1972 with the appearance of Cordelia Gray in *An Unsuitable Job for a Woman,* in which Cordelia inherits a struggling P.I. agency and a gun when her partner and mentor kills himself. Her efforts to establish the agency and support herself make the title of the book an ironic statement on society's attitudes toward a young female in an unusual line of work.

Cultural diversity is an important part of the private eye subgenre today in characters such as S. J. Rozan's Chinese American private eye Lydia Chin, who solves cases with her partner, an ex-Army brat named Bill Smith. D. B. Borton created a sixtysomething private-eye-in-training in Cat Caliban, and Sandra Scoppettone gives us hard-boiled feminist lesbian private eye Lauren Laurano. Eric Garcia's investigator isn't even human—in a blend of mystery and science fiction, he introduced a modern detective who is, actually and literally, a dinosaur. Shirley Rousseau Murphy's private eye is a talking cat named Joe Grey, and Carole Nelson Douglas's tomcat sleuth, Midnight Louie, communicates without words. Today the private investigator novel may feature a P.I. who is diverse in gender, culture, age, race, and even species.

NOIR OR NOT?

Many readers associate the hard-boiled P.I. novel with *noir,* a term derived from the French phrase *film noir,* which was used to describe the uniquely distinctive films that appeared in the forties and fifties. Film noir movies offered convoluted plots, brutal and often senseless violence, and a despairing, fatalistic vision. Confusion with the hard-boiled private eye genre occurred because some P.I. novels were made into films that are now considered film noir classics. The classic film noir list includes the movie versions of Dashiell Hammett's *The Maltese Falcon* (1941) and Raymond Chandler's *The Big Sleep* (1946). Both featured Humphrey Bogart setting the standard for hard-boiled private eyes as, respectively, Sam Spade and Philip Marlowe.

However, many film noir classics did not feature private investigators. Some examples include the film version of James M. Cain's *The Postman Always Rings Twice* (1946) and *The Killers* (1946), which was based on a short story by Ernest Hemingway. These and many other noir movies were based on what is known as "fiction noir." Many private investigator novels are noir, but not all noir fiction features private eyes. In the movies, the distinction may be blurred, but in P.I. fiction, it is less so. Hard-boiled private investigators such as Hammett's Spade and Chandler's Marlowe are tough in order to disguise their vulnerabilities. They are battered knights with a sense of honor and righteousness, however eccentric.

In fiction noir, the protagonist is usually not a detective, but a character who turns out to either be a victim, a perpetrator, or both. Nobody is innocent in fiction noir, and there are few noble characters, but instead people are blinded by desperation or avarice and enmeshed in webs created from greed, fear, and sexuality. An excellent example is *Double Indemnity,* James M. Cain's 1943 classic noir novel (made into an equally classic film noir in 1944), in which an insurance agent cannot resist the double lure of a beautiful married woman and a pile of money, seemingly easily obtainable by murdering the husband. Other authors associated with noir fiction include Jim Thompson, Cornell Woolrich, and Roald Dahl (whose noir story, *Lamb to the Slaughter,* became one of the best-known segments on the popular *Alfred Hitchcock Presents* television program).

The accepted standards of private eye fiction usually include a solitary, even a loner, detective for hire who may have a judicial or law-enforcement background but who often has an antagonistic relationship with the courts and police. Although the private eye accepts a case for a fee, altruistic and idealistic elements often enter the case. Frequently there is a sidekick or assistant, a good example of which is Archie Goodwin, who acts as Nero Wolfe's legman in Rex Stout's novels. Private eye fiction is commonly told in the first person. In other words, the reader experiences events from the point of view of the detective. Private eyes and their assistants often encounter action, sexual adventures, and extreme amounts of danger in solving their cases.

Some mystery readers do not enjoy the private detective subgenre simply because the format of this type of mystery can be less tightly structured than that of the more formally patterned, traditional mystery. This is a detail that can be discerned by doing a good readers' advisory interview (chapter 4 covers the readers' advisory interview and mystery readers).

Another point to keep in mind when suggesting this subgenre is that the amount of violence included in private eye mysteries varies greatly. Many private eye mysteries carry the tag *hard-boiled* in deference to the level of violence and amount of graphic language included in the plot. Note, however, that not all P.I. mysteries are hard-boiled. In fact, the label *soft-boiled* is used sometimes to categorize those private eye mysteries where the level of violence and graphic language has been softened and is not as prevalent in the story. Of course, there are also examples of some private eyes who could even be called *cozy*, including the classic Nero Wolfe mysteries by Rex Stout. As always, the reader's own individual tastes will dictate which private eye fiction he or she will enjoy. *(See appendix A, page 114, for a book list with some of our number-one private eyes.)*

POLICE PROCEDURAL—THEY GOT THE BEAT

Perhaps it's the fascination of watching others work that makes procedurals so popular. After all, who doesn't want to know the inside scoop? How forensic and other sciences enable the forces of law and order to bring the crime home to the perpetrator? And how the science is balanced by intuition—the "hunch"—that tells the detective that the suspect's story isn't true? A procedural offers the reader a behind-the-crime-scene look at the realities of police work. The appeal of police procedurals is durable and widespread. Look at the popularity of television shows from *Dragnet* to *N.Y.P.D. Blue*. Mystery fiction itself has millions of readers who eagerly await the next book by authors such as J. A. Jance (Seattle homicide detective J. P. Beaumont), Michael Connelly (Los Angeles homicide detective Harry Bosch), and Ian Rankin (Edinburgh inspector John Rebus).

The police procedural reader's interest in realistic methods and problems in solving crimes is piqued by the many authors whose authentic backgrounds enable them to write stories distinguished by an insider's touch. For example, Dorothy Uhnak uses the experiences garnered in her previous career as a New York policewoman to lend authenticity to her novels. Uhnak won the prestigious Edgar Award from the Mystery Writers of America (MWA) for *The Bait,* which featured Police Detective Christie Opara. Joseph Wambaugh's fourteen years as a detective sergeant in the Los Angeles Police Department give his work an unmistakable realism.

Another reason for the popularity of procedurals is that this subgenre allows the author to bring together a group of professionals working as a team, such as might be found in law-enforcement departments. The interaction of these characters' distinct personalities in both public and private settings can be explored by the author and enjoyed by fans, who avidly follow their favorite detectives through all the books in a particular series. This type of reader support for a police procedural series can be enormous. For example, author Ed McBain, whose 87th Precinct mysteries revolve around a myriad of intriguing characters, recently published the fifty-first book in that series.

Some claim that the procedural is a uniquely American subgenre, but its roots are hard to trace. Certainly British authors of the golden age, such as Ngaio Marsh, wrote mysteries featuring detective inspectors and other representatives from Scotland Yard. It can be argued, however, that Marsh's Inspector Roderick Alleyn's efforts are more like those of an amateur sleuth. The sense of a group of professionals working as a team and the authentic details are missing. Marsh's mysteries have been said to belong to the "Great Policeman" school—novels in which the actual reality of police work is omitted or ignored. Other entries in this school include Michael Innes's Inspector John Appleby.

Perhaps *Dragnet*'s L.A.P.D. Detective Joe Friday and his various partners, whose efforts to get the facts and solve crimes first appeared on radio and successfully moved to the new medium of television, might be considered as inhabiting an early procedural. Other pioneers of the procedural include Lawrence Treat, whose 1945 novel *V as in Victim* includes interdepartmental rivalries and the effects of the job on the policeman's private life, and Hillary Waugh's *Last Seen Wearing* (1952), which features on-the-job details of small-town police work. Recently, procedurals as a subgenre have been stretched to include mysteries in which a person works in an official crime-solving capacity, for example, medical examiner (such as Patricia Cornwell's Kay Scarpetta) or forensic anthropologist (such as Kathy Reichs's Temperence Brennan). Whatever this subgenre's origins, procedurals will continue to enthrall readers with the lowdown on how the professionals work.

As the readers' advisor attempts to assist a procedural reader, it is paramount to establish the reader's taste for realism and tolerance for

explicit brutality and gore. It is important to note that although a procedural reader may happily follow both Rhys Bowen's cozy Welsh
Constable Evans as well as Jon A. Jackson's tough Detroit detective
"Fang" Mulheisen, on the whole, most procedurals are distinguished by
scenes of gritty violence and an edgy tone, which some readers may find
distasteful. (For a list of our favorite police procedurals, *see* appendix A,
page 118.)

HISTORICAL SLEUTHS—CRIME THROUGH TIME

One of the fastest growing subgenres in the mystery world today is that
of the historical sleuth. Many readers look to Anne Perry, whose first historical mystery, *The Cater Street Hangman,* appeared in print in 1979;
Elizabeth Peters, who began her Amelia Peabody series with *Crocodile
on the Sandbank,* published in 1975; and Ellis Peters, who gave readers
their first glimpse of Brother Cadfael with *A Morbid Taste for Bones* in
1977, as the godmothers of this subgenre. Historical mysteries have actually been around a lot longer than this. In 1918, American writer Melville
Davisson Post offered mystery readers stories featuring the character of
Uncle Abner, a detective from the 1850s. Agatha Christie's *Death Comes
as the End,* published in 1945, featured an ancient Egyptian setting.
Lillian de la Torre's first collection of short stories with Samuel Johnson
and James Boswell appeared in print in 1948. When he was not con-
structing the perfect locked-room mystery, John Dickson Carr penned
The Bride of Newgate in 1950, just one of his books that blended mystery
with a touch of historical romance. Peter Lovesey's *Wobble to Death,*
published in 1970, introduced readers to Victorian sleuths Sergeant
Cribb and Constable Thackeray. These authors and many others set the
groundwork for the flourishing crop of historical mysteries that readers
enjoy today.

There are many reasons why mystery authors may choose to write
historical mysteries. With the advances in criminology today and the use
of such specialized techniques as DNA testing, the identity of a murderer
can now often be found simply by testing a bloodstain or matching a skin
sample. One advantage in setting a mystery in the past is that it allows
the author to put the focus of solving the crime back onto the individual
detective or sleuth. Historical sleuths are usually not able to rely simply

on science, such as fingerprint matching, to hand them their killers but instead must also employ their own wits to help solve the crime.

The past also offers many writers a different source of motives for crimes, motives that might not seem credible if used in a contemporary setting. One of the best examples of this is historical mystery writer Anne Perry, who has successfully mined the social mores and the darker side of Victorian England in a number of her books. Perry's *Brunswick Gardens* explores the clash between those who believed in the new theory of evolution and those who felt it blasphemous. *Bethlehem Road* effectively uses issues of female franchise and the rights of married women to own property as a theme in the plot. *A Sudden Fearful Death* illustrates the costs of backstreet abortions and how ignorance of birth control could lead to murder. Used in a contemporary setting, some of these issues might not pack the same emotional punch. By placing her stories in the Victorian era, Perry can illustrate the differences and similarities in their world to ours today.

Writing historical mysteries also allows some writers to play with real historical figures as characters or detectives. Peter Lovesey uses Albert Edward, the Prince of Wales, as a sleuth in one of his historical mystery series. Author George Baxt often turns to Hollywood celebrities, such as Bette Davis and Greta Garbo, who act as the detectives in his historical mysteries. Karen Harper has chosen Elizabeth I as her sleuth, and Steven Saylor put writer O. Henry to work as a detective. Other mystery writers, such as Lindsey Davis and Fiona Buckley, prefer to create their own fictional sleuths but may use historical figures as secondary characters in their stories. Writers themselves enjoy bringing these historical personages to life, and many readers also find a historical mystery to be a fun way to learn more about a real person and different time period.

The opportunity to explore the strangeness and differences of past times also draws both mystery writers and readers. For example, in Steven Saylor's *Roman Blood,* the punishment for patricide was so hideous that Saylor's sleuth, Gordianus the Finder, is driven to investigate the crime and prove the accused killer innocent. If this same crime were committed today, a contemporary detective might not feel this passion to take the case because the punishment now for this murder would be very different. Such authors as Sharan Newman and Roberta Gellis may choose a medieval setting for their mysteries because it provides the chance to explore and illuminate the struggle between the sacred and the secular worlds. This clash between two different elements of society can be quite fascinating to contemporary mystery readers, who have never faced the threat of the Inquisition or risked the displeasure of a petty tyrant but can now experience this through the magic of historical mysteries.

Authors also choose the historical mystery subgenre because of an individual expertise or interest in a certain time period. Edward Marston draws upon his extensive knowledge of Elizabethan England and the world of theater in his Nicholas Bracewell mysteries. Lynda Robinson uses her background in anthropology to capture the minute details of life in ancient Egypt in her Lord Meren series. Some authors may choose to write historical mysteries because it allows them to use a writing style that fits more comfortably with that era. Stephanie Barron drafted Jane Austen as a sleuth in her historical series, and this in turn offers Barron the opportunity to match her writing style to that of Austen herself.

Historical mystery authors do walk a fine line when it comes to how much historical detail to include in their plots and how much to leave out. Fans of this subgenre want to experience life in the past, and this is one of the most appealing elements of historical mysteries. However, when an author drenches the story in extraneous period details at the expense of the mystery plot, some readers will rebel. This balance between history and mystery can be quite a tricky thing to master.

Defining exactly what a historical mystery is and what time periods are included is perhaps the most difficult thing about the historical mystery subgenre. The Crime Writers Association, which has added an award for historical mysteries called the CWA Ellis Peters's Historical Dagger, set the cutoff date for historical mysteries eligible for the Historical Dagger as 1965. Although this offers a nice concrete date, it is by no means the only cutoff point for historical mysteries. For some readers a book is considered a historical mystery if the book's setting is at least twenty-five years prior to the book's date of publication. Then there are those readers who may have lived through a particular era, such as the Great Depression, and who might not think of Harold Adam's series or those by Fred Harris as being historical mysteries but simply mysteries.

Other readers might consider mysteries that were written as contemporary stories at the time (such as those by Sir Arthur Conan Doyle or Wilkie Collins) to be historical mysteries simply because of the passage of time since the books were written. However, *The Hound of the Baskervilles, The Woman in White,* and other books of this type are more correctly referred to as period mysteries. Fans of historical mysteries may also enjoy period mysteries.

Historical mysteries can feature a wide range of sleuths, from amateur detectives to private investigators. Although many readers will enjoy any historical mystery set in a particular time period, other readers might be picky about the type of sleuth involved. This is one thing to discuss in the readers' advisory interview. Another important caveat with this subgenre is that simply matching up books by time period does not always guarantee their appeal to an individual mystery reader. For example, numerous mystery writers, such as Allana Knight, Anne Perry, Robin Paige, Amy Lawrence, and Peter Lovesey, use the Victorian era as a setting for their books. However, individual writing styles, choices of sleuths, and settings are reasons why all of these authors will not always attract the same readers. (For some of our favorite historical mysteries, *see* appendix A, page 120.)

SUSPENSE NOVELS AND THRILLERS— SOMETHING WICKED THIS WAY COMES

Suspense novels and thrillers have their origins in the wide variety of pulp fiction and dime novels written and published in the nineteenth century. Even today this literary genre label remains imprecise and difficult to universally define. For some readers, a suspense novel conjures up images of such classics as Vera Caspary's *Laura,* Daphne du Maurier's *Rebecca,* or even John Fowles's *The Collector.* Others think of Thomas Harris's *Silence of the Lambs,* John Grisham's *The Firm,* or Joy Fielding's *See Jane Run* as the perfect thriller. The key ingredient to most suspense novels is that the protagonist's everyday, ordinary world suddenly turns menacing as he or she becomes tangled up in a life-threatening situation.

Most thrillers can be thought of as suspense novels taken to another level. In a typical suspense novel, the object of the villain's wrath is either an individual or his or her family. In many thrillers, the villain's target widens. Now, it is not just an individual who is in jeopardy, but instead it can be a whole legal system (*The Tenth Justice,* by Brad Meltzer), an entire city or country (*The First Horseman,* by John Case), or even the American way of politics (*Absolute Power*, by David Baldacci). Thrillers share many of the same elements as suspense novels, which are why they are often grouped together, but it is in the broader definition of the word *victim* that they most frequently differ.

Suspense novels and thrillers do have some key differences from mystery novels. Suspense novels are geared toward playing with the reader's emotions. Suspense writers strive to evoke feelings of fear, panic, and apprehension. Suspense readers know something dangerous is coming, and it is this feeling of terrified anticipation that they crave. Almost all mystery books have varying degrees of suspense driving their plots (as do other types of genre fiction), but mysteries primarily appeal to the reader's intellect. Mystery readers want to know who did it, how it was done, and why. With thrillers and suspense novels, it is different because the vital question now becomes how the protagonist will safely escape. Many thrillers have a cliff-hanger or episodic type of structure in which the author sets the protagonist up to face one peril only to have yet another danger waiting after that. Readers who love suspense novels and thrillers crave this roller-coaster type of read.

The ability to successfully heighten and increase the level of tension in a thriller or suspense novel is the most important skill authors in this subgenre must master. Fortunately, there are several ways of doing this. Frequently, the author puts the reader one step ahead of the main character in a suspense novel or thriller. Unable to communicate what terror lies ahead to the book's hero or heroine, the reader instead must keep turning the pages to see if and how the protagonist will escape. Many suspense and thriller authors use a variety of character viewpoints in their books to let the reader in on the villain's thoughts and plans. Compression of time also plays a role in heightening suspense. Most thrillers and suspense novels are set over a very short time period, such as a weekend, to keep the plot moving at a lightning pace.

Some suspense writers choose either a young child or young woman as a main character, because children and young women are usually the most vulnerable and innocent of victims. These types of suspense novels are sometimes referred to as *kidjep* (kids in jeopardy) or *femjep* (females in jeopardy) by publishers and readers. Another technique suspense writers can use to heighten the tension in their stories is to separate their characters from any form of help by putting them in a desolate or deserted location such as a remote mountain cabin or an isolated beach house. A perfect example of this type of character isolation is found in Mary Higgins Clark's *A Cry in the Night,* in which the heroine is trapped with the villain on an isolated farm in the Minnesota countryside. Yet another way writers can ratchet up the level of suspense in their books is by discrediting their protagonist in some way with the authorities, so that once the killer closes in, there is no hope of official help. It is up to the protagonist to stop the villain.

When it comes to novels of suspense and thrillers, pacing is everything. The key ingredient to all good thrillers is that once the reader starts the book, he or she will not want to put it down. Thus, most thrillers and suspense novels are plot driven. This does not mean that suspense writers can skip writing credible characters. Both the protagonist and the antagonist should be memorable. The protagonist should especially be someone the reader will want to root for and see succeed. But thriller and suspense writers are not given the luxury of excessive or extraneous character development. Readers who enjoy character-driven stories may find many suspense and thriller novels are not their cup of mystery tea.

Initially, it might seem that the plots of most suspense and thriller novels fall into the same pattern (e.g., innocent protagonist attempts to escape from a deranged villain), but clever writers continue to come up with new ways to twist this tried-and-true plot to their advantage. In Jessie Hunter's *One, Two, Buckle My Shoe,* the villain preys on little boys but, by mistake, snatches a little girl as his latest victim. Now the killer does not know what to do because his victim does not fall into his normal pattern. A. J. Holt's nail-biter *Watch Me* revolves around a rogue FBI agent who, upon discovering a computer chat room for serial killers, decides to eliminate all those she can trace electronically. Even though the protagonist is a killer herself in this suspense novel, readers will not care because her targets are despicably evil people. Carol O'Connell's suspense novel *Judas Child* challenges readers with the possibility that the book's ending can be read in two different ways. These are just a few examples of how talented writers are coming up with creative twists on the standard suspense plot.

The amount of violence and graphic language used in suspense and thriller fiction can vary greatly. Some suspense and thriller novelists use very little in the way of graphic violence or language in their books. The perfect example of this is the "Queen of Suspense," Mary Higgins Clark. Clark has built her reputation with readers by providing them with all the literary thrills and chills they desire sans any graphic descriptions of blood, guts, or gore. Other suspense novels, such as *Ritual,* by William Heffernan, or *The Mermaids Singing,* by Val McDermid, may not be for the squeamish reader because the descriptions of violence, although integral to the plot, can be quite intense. The level of graphic language and violence that readers will tolerate in their suspense novels and thrillers is one thing that should be clarified right at the beginning of the readers' advisory interview.

Suspense novels are frequently lumped together into one big subgenre, often referred to as psychological suspense. Most of the discussion above relates to this type of suspense novel or thriller, but you can break this subgenre down into even smaller categories, making it even easier to work with this subgenre and advise readers. Although action and adventure novels are sometimes combined into the thriller and suspense subgenre, they have some unique characteristics and have been given a section of their own in this book. (For a book list with some of our favorite suspense novels, *see* appendix A, page 124.)

LEGAL THRILLERS—WHO DOESN'T HATE A LAWYER?

The concept of lawyers in mysteries is not a new one. Charles Dickens's *Bleak House* examines the British legal system of its time, and Dorothy L. Sayers's *Strong Poison* features the trial of Harriet Vane, who has been accused of murder. Although these and other mysteries may contain lawyers in their cast of characters or have courtroom scenes, most readers do really not consider them legal thrillers today.

The Perry Mason books of Erle Stanley Gardner first successfully brought the world of the courtroom into the mystery genre. From the first Perry Mason novel, *The Case of the Velvet Claws,* published in 1933, to 1973's posthumously published *The Case of the Postponed Murder,* Gardner skillfully slipped the drama and action of the courtroom into complex detective puzzles. Both Gardner's mysteries and the TV show featuring his character Perry Mason helped create interest in the courtroom by mystery readers. Robert Traver's *Anatomy of a Murder,* which was published in 1958 and daringly included the subject of rape as part of the book's plot, also helped bring the legal world to the attention of readers.

It was Scott Turow's *Presumed Innocent* in 1987, however, that sparked the recent boom in legal thrillers, followed by John Grisham's *The Firm* in 1991. Both of these legal thrillers rocketed onto best-seller lists, and the rush by publishers and readers to find more books like these two was on. Both of these books combined the appeal of the legal profession for plot and character purposes with the fast pacing and high levels of suspense and danger associated with thrillers. This is what truly distinguishes books that are legal thrillers from those that are legal mysteries. Many mysteries, such as those by John Mortimer or Sara Woods, may use a lawyer or a judge as a sleuth or set scenes of their books in a courtroom, but if they do not have the structure and pacing of a thriller, then they are more than likely to be considered legal mysteries. A legal mystery can be an excellent read, but it probably is not what a legal thriller fan is looking for.

Critic and scholar Jon L. Breen identifies several of the major characteristics of today's legal thrillers that make them so appealing to readers (1998). Authors such as Turow, Grisham, and Steve Martini, among others, give their readers an inside look "at how the system really works." Just as fans of police procedurals enjoy gritty details in their mysteries, legal thriller readers want to know what goes on not only in the courtroom, but also behind the doors of prestigious law firms and the private chambers of judges. Unlike earlier authors such as Gardner, today's legal-eagle writers are "less likely to glorify the system" and more often use varying shades of right and wrong in their stories. Although readers are willing to give contemporary legal thriller authors more latitude in how they pursue a case, ultimately justice must still be served if the author is to be successful in this subgenre.

Grisham continues to dominate and define this subgenre for many readers—as of January 2001 there were more than sixty million copies of his books in print worldwide—but there are plenty of new authors writing legal thrillers that readers will enjoy just as much as the latest Grisham blockbuster (Maryles 2001). Brad Meltzer's first novel, *The Tenth Justice,* offers readers an intriguing look at what goes on behind the scenes of the U.S. Supreme Court as well as a terrific plot hook in that the protagonist does not know which of his friends is betraying him. William Lashner also displays a talent for crafting a superior legal thriller with his first book, *Hostile Witness,* which demonstrates that there is more than one way to see to it that justice is fulfilled. Edgar Award winner Lisa

Scottoline came up with the clever idea of using various characters from an all-women law firm as the protagonists of her legal thrillers. With authors like these, the legal thriller subgenre has a bright future ahead of itself. (Go to appendix A, page 127, for a list of our favorite legal thrillers.)

MEDICAL/BIO THRILLERS—THIS MAY HURT A BIT

"When a doctor goes wrong," Sherlock Holmes once remarked to his associate Dr. Watson, "he is the first of all criminals. He has the nerve and the knowledge." With this statement, the legendary detective illustrates the appeal of the medical thriller genre to its readers: the very people who have the skills and knowledge to prolong life can be the most effective and ruthless at ending it.

Medical mysteries of one sort or another have been published for more than 100 years. One of the earliest writers interested in mixing medicine with mystery was British author Elizabeth Thomasina Meade, whose fiction was first published in the 1890s. The first doctor to enjoy unqualified success as a mystery writer was Sir Arthur Conan Doyle, who introduced Sherlock Holmes with his 1887 publication of *A Study in Scarlet.* Doyle emphasized the use of scientific method in the pursuit of solving crimes. This opened an interesting connection between mystery and the world of science, one that other writers were quick to exploit. In addition, by using Holmes's sidekick, Dr. Watson, as the narrator of his stories, Doyle helped establish an early link between detection and the world of medicine. Doyle's books were quickly followed by the fiction of another doctor of the time, R. Austin Freeman, who also used a doctor as the narrator within his mystery stories.

In spite of the relatively long history and connections between the worlds of medicine and mystery, the use of a doctor or medical professional as a sleuth does not signify the beginning of the medical thriller subgenre itself. Medical/bio thrillers truly did not come into being until the late 1960s and early 1970s with the arrival of authors such as Robin Cook and Michael Crichton on the scene. Writing under the pseudonym Jeffrey Hudson, Crichton's first book, *A Case of Need,* was published in 1968 and went on to win an Edgar Award for best first mystery. *A Case of Need* used abortion as an important element in the book's plot, but it was Crichton's second novel, *The Andromeda Strain,* that demonstrated this author's talent for combining medical issues with the thriller format.

It was Robin Cook, however, who truly established the medical thriller subgenre with the publication of his first thriller, *Coma*, in 1977. Even today Cook continues to dominate the medical thriller subgenre, and he is usually the first name most readers associate with this type of book. With two exceptions, *Sphinx* and *Abduction*, Cook's books display all the elements of the medical thriller subgenre that appeal to its readers. First of all, the book focuses on a mysterious medical crisis, and the solution to the mystery is tied back into the field of medicine or science. Cook's thrillers employ an impressive amount of research, but the research is carefully distilled into an entertaining plot. Cook also has a knack for choosing a topic that seems to have been snatched from the latest newspaper headlines. A top-notch medical/bio thriller employs a current topic, the research and industry knowledge needed to back up the plot, and a story that focuses on the medical milieu. As with all types of thrillers, a fast-paced story is also a necessity.

Although Cook many reign as the king of the medical/bio thriller, he does have some serious competition from other writers. Novelists such as Tess Gerritsen and Michael Palmer are using their medical knowledge to pen some of the most frightening tales of medical terror. Inspirational and Christian fiction writers have also embraced this subgenre, though with one major difference: most Christian medical thrillers are not written by doctors or those in the medical profession. One example of this is Alton Gansky, a pastor, whose *By My Hands* and *Marked for Mercy* are billed as medical suspense by their publisher.

Medical/bio thrillers seem to be right on the cutting edge when it comes to following societal trends. Whatever the current hot topic is in the real world of science—fetal tissue research, the Ebola virus, genetic tinkering, illegal organ transplants, and so forth—you can be sure it will turn up in the pages of these exciting thrillers. (Appendix A, page 129, has a book list with our favorite medical/bio thrillers.)

ROMANTIC SUSPENSE—DEADLY KISSES AND PERILOUS PASSION

"A man, a woman, a puzzle, terrible danger, and yes, raging hormones." Author Eileen Dreyer (aka Kathleen Korbel) succinctly summarizes the major components of today's romantic suspense novels, because, in its most perfect form, romantic suspense is an equal blend of romance and mystery (1997, 152). Therefore, this is a subgenre that is claimed by both mystery and romance readers. The appeal to readers is its dual nature: romantic suspense promises a story that focuses both on the developing relationship between the hero and heroine as well as on the thrill of danger and excitement, all with a happy ending. The romantic suspense subgenre offers a range of reading choices—from the classic, beautifully atmospheric tales of Mary Stewart to the sizzling suspense novels of Sandra Brown and Jayne Ann Krentz. This seductive combination of passion and danger is a potent lure for many readers.

The roots of romantic suspense grow deep. Nineteenth-century literary classics, such as *The Mysteries of Udolpho*, by Ann Radcliffe, *Wuthering Heights*, by Emily Brontë, and *Jane Eyre*, by Charlotte Brontë, are often cited as the foundation for the gothic and romantic suspense novels of the twentieth century. The early twentieth century gave rise to a new label for this type of book: Had I But Known. Although critics often sneeringly applied this label to denigrate this subgenre, it more correctly is a reflection of a writing technique used by authors such as Mary Roberts Rinehart and Mignon G. Eberhart. In 1938, one of the true classics of romantic suspense was published: Daphne du Maurier's masterpiece, *Rebecca*, which delighted readers and would become a source of literary inspiration for a new generation of romantic suspense writers.

Readers' advisors may find romantic suspense's sister subgenre, gothics, grouped together with romantic suspense, but gothics have their own unique characteristics, and they really deserve a subgenre of their own. Most often set in the past, with a story centered in one location, gothics are all about atmosphere. Gothic novels ruled the publishing world during the 1960s and 1970s, and authors such as Victoria Holt and Madeleine Brent gained a tremendous following. Just as all literary trends change, so too have gothics given way in popularity to the romantic suspense novels of today, though the occasional gothic touch can still be discerned in some authors currently writing romantic suspense, such as Kay Hooper.

Although some mystery aficionados may scoff at romantic suspense's place in the mystery genre, other mystery critics and readers have recognized its true worth. Mary Stewart was awarded the British

Crime Writer's Association's Silver Dagger for *My Brother Michael* in 1961, and two other of her romantic suspense novels were nominated for the Mystery Writers of America's Edgar Award. Several of the Mystery Writers of America's Grandmaster Award winners have also come from this subgenre, among them Phyllis A. Whitney and Eberhart. Recently, *Rebecca* swept past a distinguished field of other mystery titles to win the Anthony Award as Best Novel of the Century.

Today, romance writers such as Jayne Ann Krentz (whose book *Soft Focus* is almost an homage to film noir), Linda Howard, and Nora Roberts have turned to writing romantic suspense, thus effectively broadening their readership and bringing romance readers into the mystery genre. Novels by these and other authors frequently turn up on national best-seller lists, yet another indication of their popularity with readers and the important place romantic suspense has in the world of mysteries. (For some of our favorite romantic suspense novels, *see* appendix A, page 133.)

ACTION AND ADVENTURE—
TESTOSTERONE-DRENCHED TALES

Tales of heroic quests, stories of men in combat, novels of survival, books filled with swashbuckling deeds and derring-do—all of these and more fit comfortably under the action and adventure subgenre. The action and adventure subgenre itself can be a bit confusing for the novice readers' advisor because it does incorporate so many different types of books and because boundaries between the various kinds of action and adventure novels can easily become blurred. Although some types of action and adventure books, such as military adventure novels, are easy to distinguish and practically form their own separate subset, other action and adventure novels may fall into several different categories of this subgenre.

Action and adventure stories staked their place in literature early on. From Homer's rousing seafaring adventure, *The Odyssey,* to the heroic escapades of King Arthur's Knights of the Roundtable, stories whose plots contained a good dose of action have always been popular with readers. Books that today are labeled classic literature, such as Jack London's *Call of the Wild,* Daniel Defoe's *The Life and Adventures of*

Robinson Crusoe, and Robert Louis Stevenson's *Treasure Island,* were actually popular action and adventure tales of their day. Many well-known mystery writers have also turned out the occasional action and adventure story, including Sir Arthur Conan Doyle, whose historical adventure tale, *The White Company,* can be classified in this subgenre.

Although suspense and thriller books and action and adventure novels are often mixed in together and share some similarities, there are some distinct differences between these subgenres. Thrillers and suspense books usually have a more twisted, byzantine plot structure. The reader frequently knows the identity of the villain in a thriller, although the protagonist usually does not, thus generating a significant portion of the suspense in the plot. The identity of the villain in action and adventure novels is often no secret to either the reader or the book's protagonist. In some cases, the action and adventure "villain" may not even be a real person, such as the earthquake that dominates the plot of Peter Hernon's *8.4.*

Action and adventure novels are often considered the provenance of male readers and writers. In fact, some critics have termed this subgenre as "wish fulfillment for males," but this just is not true. Female readers can and do enjoy action and adventure stores just as much as their male counterparts. Even though male protagonists may still be the rule rather than the exception in this subgenre, authors such as Wilbur Smith and Douglas J. Preston and Lincoln Child write strong female characters into their books, which are in turn equally appealing to readers of both sexes. As with any readers' advisory interaction, do not assume that someone will not be interested in a particular genre simply because of his or her gender.

Readers love action and adventure fiction for the same reason that their nonfiction counterparts like Sebastian Junger's *The Perfect Storm* and Jon Krakauer's *Into Thin Air* are experiencing a resurgence in popularity. This subgenre celebrates the triumph of an ordinary individual or group over seemingly insurmountable obstacles. For readers who have never had firsthand experience with war or gone hand to hand with Mother Nature, these books fill a need to vicariously experience life on the edge. Action and adventure novels come in many flavors, and this is part of their appeal to readers. Action and adventure novels can take a historical turn with a series such as the Flashman books, by George MacDonald Fraser, or the Horatio Hornblower stories of C. S. Forester. Other action and adventure novels focus on plots in which a variety of natural disasters ranging from tsunamis to volcanoes must be faced. Still other action and adventure novels have a military slant, such as many of Jack Higgins's books or many of W. E. B. Griffin's titles.

It is not always easy to separate some military action and adventure books from their techno-thriller cousins because both have many of the same characteristics. One rule of thumb to follow is that if the use of gadgets in the plot is secondary to the characters themselves, then the book is probably an action and adventure story, but if the gadgets and equipment are more important, it's probably a techno-thriller.

Whether it is the classic adventure tales of authors such as Alistair MacLean or Hammond Innes or the latest crop of titles like *Ice Station,* by Matthew J. Reilly, and *Torchlight,* by Robert Louis Stevenson III, action and adventure readers have a wealth of choices that will satisfy their appetite for excitement and adventure. (Our favorite action and adventure books can be found in appendix A, page 136.)

TECHNO-THRILLERS—BOYS AND THEIR TOYS

An offshoot of the action and adventure genre, the techno-thriller focuses on high-tech scenarios and features plots rife with thrilling near misses, courageous and daring feats of action, and an extremely fast-paced story line. Frequently, techno-thrillers conclude with a "countdown" type of climactic ending, and their plots often center on the military or national security interests. By definition, the techno-thriller also shares some characteristics with the thriller genre; for instance, the pace of the story should be quick and unrelenting. There is the same sense of urgency in reading techno-thrillers as other types of thrillers in that the reader, once he or she begins the book, feels compelled to finish the story.

A good techno-thriller revolves around technology—it must be an integral and inseparable part of the plot woven so closely into the story line that if taken out, the book falls apart. Some form of technology must permeate the story and be crucial to the story's evolution and conclusion. In fact, whatever form of technology that is used, be it weapons, computers, or electronics, becomes so important to the story and its readers that it becomes a character in and of itself. This focus on technology is part of this subgenre's appeal to its readers.

Techno-thriller writers face some unique demands when they begin plotting their latest books, and the most important factor that comes into play is attention to detail. Techno-thriller writers must get all their facts straight when it comes to the form of technology that inhabits their plots. The tiniest error can cause a reader to lose interest in the story and discredit the author. Because many techno-thrillers have a military setting, it is not surprising that a significant portion of techno-thriller writers come from a military background. Authors such as Dale Brown and Stephen Coonts use their insider's knowledge to lend authenticity to their stories. However, one interesting exception to this rule is Tom Clancy, who relies on his extensive research to substitute for any former connection to the armed forces.

As with other subgenres, the boundary lines for techno-thrillers are not always clear-cut. Some authors, such as Clive Cussler, may borrow elements of the techno-thriller—in Cussler's case it is a love of machines such as planes, ships, or vintage cars—and fuse these techno elements onto a traditional action and adventure plot. Clancy has adopted components of the political thriller and even the espionage subgenre to liven up his stories.

Although the last two decades have seen a rise in the popularity of the techno-thriller, with writers such as Clancy leading the pack, the subgenre is not really a new one. Elements of techno-thrillers have actually been around for at least 100 years or more, although the term may not have been used for books at that time. Authors such as Jules Verne often filled their novels with the latest in real or imagined technology (think of the submarine *Nautilus* from *Twenty Thousand Leagues under the Sea*). Children's book series like Tom Swift displayed a fascination for anything scientific that the hero could use in his fights or explorations. Then there is Edward L. Beach's classic World War II novel, *Run Silent, Run Deep,* whose submarine warfare plot is the precursor to Clancy's *The Hunt for Red October.*

Clancy himself initially insisted that he did not invent the techno-thriller subgenre (Coonts 1990, 18). In fact, for a long time Clancy stated that he wrote political thrillers and totally rejected the application of the term *techno-thriller* to his works. Clancy often points to Michael Crichton's *The Andromeda Strain,* which is also claimed by devotees of the medical thriller for their subgenre, as the first real techno-thriller. However, when Clancy's first book, *The Hunt for Red October,* was published, reviewers found the technical aspects of the novel so impressive and unusual, a new word had to be coined to describe this type of reading experience, and thus the term *techno-thriller* was born.

Techno-thriller writers have a wide range of options to choose from when dreaming up the plots of their latest books. The technology woven into their stories can come from almost anywhere, whether it is the bathyscaphes and Autosubs that explore deep beneath the ocean's surface or the cutting-edge space stations that flirt with the edges of outer space. All forms of nuclear weaponry, assorted missiles, various types of aircraft, and even computers themselves can play important roles in the plots of techno-thrillers, and current events, such as the imagined Y2K crisis, can offer themselves up as fodder for the writer's imagination. By combining the technology of both the present and the future with a dramatic plot and a fast-paced narrative, techno-thriller writers are giving their readers exactly what they want. (For a list of terrific techno-thrillers, *see* appendix A, page 138.)

ESPIONAGE—DIRTY SECRETS
AND DOUBLE AGENTS

Writers and readers have long been fascinated by what Rudyard Kipling termed the "great game" in his novel *Kim.* Spies have played minor roles in literature for centuries. The Bible records several incidents of spying, and Homer employs the occasional bit of espionage in his writing. Although James Fenimore Cooper's 1821 novel, *The Spy: A Tale of the Neutral Ground,* is considered to be the first American espionage novel, espionage fiction really did not emerge as a separate category in and of itself until the early 1900s. At first, the Germans were the predominant villains of spy novels, and works such as Erskine Childer's *The Riddle of the Sands* capitalized on this trend. The rise of Communism in the 1920s gave birth to a new category of villains, as did the growing Nazi threat of the 1930s.

After World War II, the cold war played a major role in most spy novels. With the breakup of the former USSR, many spy novelists are scouting new avenues for ideas. Authors such as Richard Harris, with his book *Enigma;* John Altman, with his thriller *A Gathering of Spies;*

Daniel Silva's *The Unlikely Spy;* Alan Furst's *Night Soldiers;* and Ken Follett's classic, *Eye of the Needle,* have turned to the past (in these cases, the World War II era) for inspiration. Meanwhile, the murky morals of industrial and economic espionage are proving to be a fertile source of plots for other contemporary espionage writers. The rise of China to prominence in world politics also promises a new interest in the East as a setting and a geopolitical villain capable of replacing the Soviets.

For a long time espionage was thought to be a man's game, and espionage fiction mirrored this sentiment. Male authors and male protagonists dominated this subgenre. With few exceptions, if a woman was allowed into the plot of a spy novel, she was usually either cast in the role of a Mata Hari or the love interest of the male protagonist, such as the many women who graced James Bond's bed. The first female author to successfully crack the espionage genre was Helen MacInnes, whose first book, *Above Suspicion,* debuted in 1941. MacInnes's protagonists, both male and female, were most often amateurs who become caught up in the terrifying world of international intrigue. Then came Peter O'Donnell's creation, Modesty Blaise, who rose above her orphaned childhood to become the leader of an international crime ring, only to retire from her life of crime and become an agent for a supersecret British agency. From the first book in which Modesty appeared, 1965's *Modesty Blaise,* through the succeeding novels, comic strips, and film, this was one woman who was more than equal to any male spy out in the field. Today's readers have quite a number of what one clever bookseller dubbed as "Jane Bonds" to choose from, including Maureen Tan's excellent series featuring MI5 agent Jane Nichols, as well as Francine Mathews's *Cutout,* which draws upon the author's own knowledge of the spy biz. Readers with a sense of humor will want to give Mabel Maney's *The Spy Who Came Out of the Closet* a try, because its heroine is really Jane Bond, James Bond's lesbian twin sister.

Espionage fiction appeals to readers for many different reasons. For some, it is the promise of secrets waiting to be revealed. There is also a thrill in knowing that certain authors bring their own insider knowledge to their plots. For other readers, it is the lure of exotic locales, slinky femmes fatales, dangerously evil villains, and colorful displays of heroic action. Espionage fiction offers readers the danger and intrigue they crave by thrusting them into a world where nothing is what it seems and where no one can be trusted. As Michael Cox points out in his introduction to

The Oxford Book of Spy Stories (1997, xi), "The world of the spy story is, by definition, founded on deception, betrayal, and duplicity. But at the same time it is also one in which patriotism, duty, and selfless sacrifice supply the springs of action." This dual nature of espionage fiction is perhaps its strongest attraction for readers. It's a Machiavellian genre in which the end justifies the means and characters must continuously reconcile their individual moral and ethical choices with larger issues of national safety and political ideologies.

As with many other mystery subgenres, espionage fiction can be difficult to define simply because it has so many permutations. Authors such as W. Somerset Maugham, Joseph Conrad, and Graham Greene bring the spy novel into the realms of literature, while paperback series featuring characters such as Matt Helm and Nick Carter push it closer to the world of pulp fiction. Depending on the author, espionage fiction can either glorify the sacrifices made in the name of the game or point out the double-dealing and double standards that become second nature for so many fictional spies. From Dorothy Gilman's cozy Mrs. Pollifax series to the darker, more graphic games of intrigue played out in books by Robert Ludlum and David Morrell, there is literally something for almost every espionage reader to enjoy. (For a book list with some of our favorite espionage stories, *see* appendix A, page 141.)

TRUE CRIME—DOES PAY

Most readers' advisory work concentrates on fiction, but with the mystery genre one must also consider true crime books as part of the spectrum of choices open to the mystery reader. True crime books provoke strong reactions: some readers will not touch this type of book with a ten-foot pole, yet others cannot get enough of this subgenre. The Mystery Writers of America recognizes true crime's place in the mystery genre by including a "Fact Crime" category of Edgar Awards. Another reason to keep the true crime subgenre in mind when practicing your mystery readers' advisory skills is that some very popular mystery authors, including P. D. James, Edna Buchanan, Barbara D'Amato, Lois Duncan, James Ellroy, and Ann Rule, have written both mystery fiction and nonfiction. Readers' advisory staff should be prepared for the small but enthusiastic group of readers who will appreciate your recommendations in this subgenre.

What draws readers to true crime books? Some experts feel that it is because these books explore the darkest corners of our psyches and attempt to give some meaning or context to horrible crimes. True crime aficionados are fascinated by the extremes of human behavior, illustrating that the world's real murderers are more twisted and fiendish than any villain or predator dreamed up for the pages of a novel. Most of all, true crime readers want to know why these people turned into such monsters. What is it that can make a seemingly normal person morph into a deranged killer? Is there some clue or some similar sign that readers can watch for in their own lives to help keep themselves and their families safe?

Books about true crimes have been popular with readers and sought after by publishers ever since Truman Capote's *In Cold Blood* became a best-seller in 1966. Capote, then a well-established and celebrated novelist, became intrigued by the story of Herb Clutter, a wealthy Kansas farmer, who was murdered in his home along with his wife and two children. Capote was inspired to drive to Kansas, where he intended to do some research and write an article for the *New Yorker,* but he became so caught up in the murders that for years it was all he could think about. When Random House published *In Cold Blood,* it brought attention to the true crime genre that has never been equaled. It helped that the form of the book itself was controversial because Capote insisted he had done something entirely unique—he created the "nonfiction novel." Whatever it is called, Capote had written the best true crime book to date.

In Cold Blood was followed by subsequent true crime best-sellers such as *Helter Skelter; The Boston Strangler; Nutcracker: Money, Madness, and Murder; At Mother's Request;* and *Fatal Vision,* to name just a few. These titles also indicate that within the true crime subgenre there is a distinct range of books. As publisher Lou Aronica of Bantam points out, "There are very literate studied pieces like Joe McGinniss's work and then there are the far more lurid, *National Enquirer* kind of projects. They sell equally well but I cannot believe that the same readers turn to both" (Blades 1995).

Most successful true crime books have the following common factors: the subject of the book is a contemporary crime, the crime is most frequently murder, and there is an official investigation and usually a trial. With a few rare exceptions of subjects such as Jack the Ripper,

Lizzie Borden, Stanford White, and the Lindbergh kidnapping, publishers and readers generally are not looking for books that focus on historical crimes. The best true crime books involve thorough research on the part of the author. The acknowledged masters of this field, such as Jack Olsen, Joe McGinniss, and Ann Rule, all read trial transcripts several times in addition to doing extensive interviews with everyone involved in the case.

Just as important as the research to authors is their choice of criminals. There must be something about the criminal that will fascinate the reader. Is he handsome and charming like Jeffrey MacDonald? Is he a seemingly successful husband, father, and physician like Sam Sheppard? True crime authors spend as much time selecting the subjects of their books as mystery writers spend creating their protagonists.

The victim is equally important to true crime readers and writers. One of the reasons Ann Rule is so successful as a true crime writer is her compassion for the people she writes about. Rule herself acknowledges, "I am aware of the fact that I make a living writing about other people's tragedies" (Ryan 1991, 54). Rule tries very hard to get to know the victims so that she can see and feel their pain. The more the author is able to unlock the personalities of the key players in the crime, the more likely the reader is to become involved in the story.

Rule also understands the appeal of her books to readers. In an article for *Good Housekeeping* magazine, Rule said the response she gives to many of her fans who ask if they might not be weird because they are fascinated by true crime books is, "None of us can understand why anyone would deliberately hurt another living being. That's why I write about murderers—because I have to know why. And that's why you read my books. It's the gentlest of us who are most intrigued" (Rule 1991, 42).

Since the publication of *In Cold Blood,* true crime books have always been a part of the literary landscape, but there are indications that this might be changing. The rise in the number of reality-based television police shows and the saturation of the television news shows by tabloid-type productions may have put a dent in the number of true crime books published. A recent trend tied into this subgenre is the interest in publishers and readers in titles that focus on criminology or forensics. Books such as *Mindhunter: Inside the FBI's Elite Serial Crimes Unit,* by John E. Douglas and Mark Olshaker, Ted Conover's *Newjack: Guarding Sing Sing,* and *Dead Men Do Tell Tales: The Strange and*

Fascinating Cases of a Forensic Anthropologist, by Michael Browning and William R. Maples, are just a few examples of this type of nonfiction. These books may not fit the traditional scope of the true crime genre, yet they are something that savvy mystery readers' advisors need to keep in mind.

Although true crime books are nonfiction, for many of their fans, the best examples of this subgenre read like fiction. This presents the opportunity for readers' advisory staff to cross sell some of these books to fiction readers. Thriller and suspense fiction fans will find that many true crime books contain the same page-turning, suspenseful elements they crave. Fans of police procedurals will discover that many true crime writers devote a considerable amount of their books to following the official investigation and how the police or other government agencies nab their killers. Some true crime books also spend a good amount of time covering the trial of the killer, and this might lure in devotees of legal thrillers. Being a good readers' advisor means being aware of all of the possible types of books your readers might be intrigued by, and for mystery readers' advisory work, this means adding true crime to your repertoire of choices. (Appendix A, page 144 has a list with some of our favorite true crime books.)

ANTHOLOGIES—COLLECTIONS OF MYSTERY MORSELS

The popularity of mystery short story collections is greater than you might suspect, although librarians do not often think to recommend an anthology when doing readers' advisory work. Readers enjoy anthologies because it is easy to pick up a collection, read a story, and then put it down again for further reading as time permits. Anthologies are also a quick way to try out the work of several different authors. Often a reader will discover a particular author through his or her work in an anthology, prompting the reader to follow that author's work from the short story format to his or her novels.

Many mystery anthologies are compiled around a "hook." These can include such themes as certain locales, historical periods, animals, holidays—the list is endless. For example, pet lovers dig right into anthologies such as *Hound Dunnit and Cat Crimes*. Indeed, when the latter anthology was introduced, its immediate popularity led to a connected series of cat-and-crime-themed anthologies, including *Cat Crimes II and Cat Crimes III* as well as *Cat Crimes through Time* and *Feline and Famous: Cat Crimes Goes Hollywood.*

Although some mystery writers may pick an entirely different character and type of mystery for their short stories, as opposed to their mystery novels, other writers choose to use their familiar sleuths in a short story setting. Examples of the latter include Peter Tremayne's historical detective Sister Fidelman, Agatha Christie's Tommy and Tuppence, and Steven Saylor's Gordianus the Finder. All of these characters have graced both mystery novels and short stories. G. K. Chesterton's Father Brown and Lillian de La Torre's Dr. Sam Johnson are just two examples of sleuths who have only appeared in short stories.

Genre short stories have always attracted readers, but it was the pulp magazine industry that really increased their popularity. Pulp magazines, which flourished between the early 1920s and the late 1950s, offered all kinds of stories, including mystery short stories. Readers liked the format and the accessibility of these magazines, which exclusively catered to popular reading tastes. Though the pulps themselves eventually ceased to be published, other mystery and detective story magazines continue to be popular with readers today, publishing stories by some of the genre's most highly regarded authors.

Perhaps the two most venerable magazines catering to the mystery short story reader are *Ellery Queen's Mystery Magazine,* first published in 1941, and *Alfred Hitchcock's Mystery Magazine,* which appeared on the scene in 1956. The indefatigable team of Manfred B. Lee and Frederic Dannay, jointly known as "Ellery Queen," edited *Ellery Queen's Mystery Magazine.* In addition to writing the mystery series featuring their popular amateur detective Ellery Queen, Lee and Dannay edited the magazine until their respective deaths, in 1971 and 1982. *Ellery Queen's Mystery Magazine* continues on under editor Janet Hutchings. *Alfred Hitchcock's Mystery Magazine* was never actually edited by the great director himself but benefited from his famous name. It was originally edited by William Manners and is currently edited by Cathleen Jordan. Apart from mystery short story anthologies, these and other genre magazines are often the source for many of the mystery short stories nominated for awards from the various mystery associations. Many of the best-known mystery awards, such as the Agatha, the Edgar, and the Shamus, include a category for short stories.

Savvy librarians know that even old and battered copies of mystery anthologies, such as *Ellery Queen's Aces of Mystery* and *Alfred Hitchcock Presents Stories That Scared Even Me,* will pay for the cost and effort of mending and rebinding with continued high circulations. More recent mystery anthologies are equally appealing to readers, proving that a large and diverse collection of mystery short story anthologies should be a part of any mystery fiction collection. (Go to appendix A, page 147, for a list of short story collections we loved.)

GENREBLENDED MYSTERIES— TORN BETWEEN TWO GENRES

One of the most significant trends affecting readers' advisory work is the blending and blurring of fiction genres. Mystery fiction is no exception to this trend. Thus, a category of genreblended mysteries is often needed for readers' advisory work. Genreblended mysteries borrow elements from a number of other fiction genres such as fantasy, horror, and science fiction. The one common element that these genreblended mysteries have is that the mystery component of the plot is strong enough to attract a mystery reader.

When the blurring between two genres becomes commonplace enough to attract a considerable number of writers and readers, a new subgenre arises. Romantic suspense has brought together elements from the romance genre with the mystery and suspense genre for a good portion of the twentieth century. Historical mysteries owe their origins to both the historical novel and mystery genres. Although both of these subgenres may have started out as experiments on the part of a few authors who wanted to try something new and different, now they have a permanent place in the world of mysteries.

Although the craze for genreblended books seems to be a recent one, these types of books have actually been around for many years. Science fiction and fantasy have incorporated elements from the mystery genre for a long time. Sir Arthur Conan Doyle's classic 1912 Professor Challenger tale, *The Lost World,* mixed science fiction with an adventure novel. This in turn would later inspire contemporary science fiction writer Greg Bear in 1998 to write *Dinosaur Summer,* a blend of historical fiction, adventure, and science fiction. Beginning with his 1954 book, *The Caves of Steel,* author Isaac Asimov introduced readers to the concept of a robot detective. Author Randall Garrett is known by both fantasy and mystery readers for his acclaimed Lord Darcy series, which distilled elements of fantasy and detective fiction into three delightful novels as well as several short stories, beginning with *Too Many Magicians,* published in 1967. More recently, Terry Pratchett spoofed the hard-boiled detective genre, among other things, in *Men at Arms,* one of his popular Discworld novels.

Western fiction and mysteries have also cross-pollinated one another with interesting results for decades. This really is not surprising because both these genres focus on the triumph of justice and the restoration of order. Several Louis L'Amour westerns used a strong mystery to anchor the plot. Western writer James Warner Bellah's 1960 book, *Sergeant Rutledge,* features a buffalo soldier who is charged with double homicide and assault and must find the real killer to clear his name. In 1979, author Loren Estleman wrote *The High Rocks,* which became the first book in his series featuring "western cop" Page Murdock. Award-winning mystery writer Bill Pronzini achieved almost the perfect combination of the western and mystery genres with his book *Quincannon,* while Bill Crider, another mystery writer who also authors westerns, has several genre-blurred books, including *Ryan Rides Back.* Best-selling mystery writer Tony Hillerman's *Skinwalkers* won not only the Anthony Award for best mystery, but also garnered the Golden Spur Award from the Western Writers of America for Best Western Novel, demonstrating that critics of both genres know a good book when they read it.

The blending of horror or paranormal elements into a mystery has also attracted inventive authors. J. S. Le Fanu, whose first collection of short stories, in 1851, included both ghost and mystery tales, is known for his story "Green Tea," which blended the supernatural and the mysterious. William Hope Hodgson's psychic detective and ghost finder Carnacki debuted in 1913 with the book *Carnacki the Ghost Finder.* Popular writer Barbara Michaels used a pinch of the paranormal in several of her suspense novels, including *Ammie Come Home* and *Patriot's Dream.* Richard Matheson gave readers a time-travel mystery with *Somewhere in Time.* Barbara Hambly, who writes in several genres, managed to successfully combine historical fiction, horror, and a mystery in her classic, *Those Who Hunt the Night.*

The trend for blending horror or the paranormal and mystery continues. Laurell Hamilton has attracted a strong readership, including many mystery readers, to her horror series featuring vampire hunter Anita Blake. Fantasy author Tanya Huff paired her police officer turned private detective with her very own vampire partner in a series of books that began with *Blood Price.* Thomas Harris's books focusing on serial killer Hannibal Lecter are enjoyed by both mystery and horror readers. Mystery writer Martha Lawrence has developed a popular and critical reputation for her "woo-woo" mystery series starring parapsychologist-turned-private-investigator Elizabeth Chase.

Even literary fiction is not immune to the lure of the mystery genre. Margaret Atwood's *Alias Grace,* Alice Hoffman's *The River King,* Lauren Belfer's *City of Light,* David Guterson's *Snow Falling on Cedars,* and Jodi Piccolt's *Plain Truth* are just a few examples of literary fiction writers who have included everything from a pinch to a good measure of mystery to their stories. Interestingly enough, some literary fiction readers are awakening to the fact that many mystery writers, such as Sharon McCrumb, James Lee Burke, and Margaret Maron, have distinct literary voices and unique writing styles and their books can be enjoyed for the prose as well as the intrigue.

Genreblended mysteries appeal to readers because they promise something different and slightly exotic. Because these genreblended books offer some of the same elements of a genre the reader is familiar with and enjoys, in this case mysteries, they also may not be as threatening for the reader to try. Yet the greatest appeal of these books for readers also presents the greatest challenge to readers' advisors. Where do you draw genre lines? In addition, the amount of genreblending tolerated will vary greatly from reader to reader.

One of the best things about genreblended mysteries is that they offer readers' advisory staff an easy means of introducing the mystery genre to readers who might not pick up a mystery on their own. Conversely, adding genreblended mysteries to your fiction collection may also push traditional mystery readers into exploring and enjoying other genres, such as science fiction. Think of genre-blurred mysteries as adding spice to your library's collection. They can be the perfect way to pique the jaded reading tastes of those who might be bored with their usual choices. (Appendix A, page 150, has a list of some of our favorite genre blends.)

4

Mystery Readers and the Readers' Advisory Interview

One of the key ingredients to most successful readers' advisory interactions is the readers' advisory interview. All library staff who provide readers' advisory service should be familiar with the second edition of Joyce G. Saricks and Nancy Brown's *Readers' Advisory Service in the Public Library* (1997). The authors offer a brilliant introduction to the principles of readers' advisory service; their insight into discovering the appeal of a book and the basics of a readers' advisory interview form the foundation for providing good readers' advisory service in any library.

Saricks's *Readers' Advisory Guide to Genre Fiction* (2001) serves as an excellent companion to *Readers' Advisory Service in the Public Library*. Adventure, mysteries, suspense, and thrillers are among the fiction genres covered by Saricks, who provides important characteristics of each genre, suggests readers' advisory interview tips, and offers ideas of key authors and reference sources.

The appeal of a book to a reader is not only a matter of which genre or subgenre the book falls into, but also depends on other characteristics of the book itself. Successful mystery readers' advisory work is not simply a case of providing readers with a listing of assorted mystery writers by subgenre, but in also knowing how the various appeal factors of an individual mystery title can affect a reader. As outlined by Saricks and

Brown, these appeal factors can be the book's pace, type of characterization, story line, and frame of the story. Once you have mastered the basics suggested by Saricks and Brown, it is easier to see how these elements transfer from a broad level to an individual fiction genre such as the mystery and even to a single book.

For example, the mystery reader who loves Mary Higgins Clark's *Weep No More My Lady* may or may not like Chris Mooney's *Deviant Ways*. Both books fall into the suspense subgenre, but Mooney's book is far more graphic in terms of violence. The story line of *Deviant Ways* might not appeal to a reader who enjoys Clark's softer suspense novels. The reader looking for a classic British police procedural by an author like Clare Curzon might find Elizabeth George's series featuring Inspector Thomas Lynley and Sergeant Barbara Havers to be overdone and overwrought. In this case, the pacing in George's books may be too leisurely, the level of description too much. The only way we as readers' advisors can find these things out is through the readers' advisory interview.

A necessary part of the readers' advisory interview is geared toward getting readers to share examples of authors and titles they have enjoyed in the attempt to find similar books that will appeal to the reader. However, don't rely solely on a reader's prior choices when it comes time to suggest new authors and titles. Part of the readers' advisory interview should also focus on what the reader might be in the mood for right now. Authors Catherine Sheldrick Ross and Mary K. Chelton (2001) demonstrate that a reader's present mood is as important to the readers' advisory interview as what they have enjoyed reading in the past.

Let's take, as an example, a reader who loves legal thrillers by authors such as John Grisham and Steve Martini but who may now be burned out on that particular subgenre. In this case, if the reader is still looking for a fast-paced story with a good measure of suspense, you might suggest David Baldacci's political thriller *Absolute Power* or even *Nest of Vipers,* by Linda Davies, which is set against the banking industry. Both have similar appeal elements in terms of pacing and suspense levels but different settings, which might be exactly what the reader is now in the mood for.

Mystery readers give us many clues when they talk about their favorite authors or the type of book they prefer to read. The readers who say they enjoy a page-turner or a fast-paced type of read are probably more likely to appreciate something from the suspense or thriller sub-genres instead of a cozy amateur sleuth mystery. The reader who states he loves Sue Grafton's Kinsey Millhone series because he likes following the character from book to book may be telling you that he prefers a mystery series rather than a title that stands alone. By encouraging readers to talk about what they like and dislike and even what they want to read now, you will get a better idea of what type of mysteries may appeal to them. Figure 1 lists useful questions to ask in the readers' advisory interview.

Although we like to think that all readers are eagerly waiting to engage in a dialogue with us about their favorite books, the truth is that some readers are not used to or comfortable with the whole readers' advisory interview concept. These readers may hover on the fringes of

---

FIGURE 1
Checklist for a Mystery Readers' Advisory Interview

_____ Determine if the reader has a preference for a certain subgenre of mystery.

_____ Discern what elements appeal the most to the reader. Is it mood, writing style, setting, type of character, or flow of the mystery?

_____ How much violence, graphic language, and sex is the reader comfortable with in a mystery?

_____ Does the reader express a preference for a certain gender of sleuth?

_____ What about mysteries appeal the most to the reader: solving the puzzle, finding a protagonist they can relate to, or a certain theme in a mystery?

_____ Does the reader have a fondness for series?

_____ Does the author write under other names? Remember that authors may use pseudonyms and that some readers will enjoy reading all of an author's work, no matter whose name is on the book's cover.

---

your fiction collection like shy woodland creatures just waiting to bolt. Others may brusquely reject any offer to help them find something to read. The key to good readers' advisory service is to match the level of service you offer to the individual reader. The shy reader may need several visits before he or she feels ready to actively participate in a conversation with a readers' advisor. Therefore, ease up on the third-degree readers' advisory interview and just let this reader know there are staff available who would be happy to provide some reading suggestions. The reader who rejects any offer of assistance by staff may prefer a more passive form of readers' advisory service such as book lists or a display. The readers' advisory interview—indeed, the whole readers' advisory experience—is not a one-size-fits-all kind of service.

Each fiction genre seems to have its own particular issue that must be taken into account when it comes to the readers' advisory interview. For the romance genre, the issue is the amount of sensuality with which the reader feels comfortable. With the mystery genre, the question is how much violence—and, to a lesser extent, graphic language and sex—is acceptable to the reader? Readers' comfort levels as to the graphic language, violence, and sex contained in a mystery will vary greatly. Finding a graceful way to introduce this topic into the readers' advisory interview is not always easy. After all, no one wants to be thought of either as a wimp or as some kind of deviant who thrills to bloody scenes of violence.

There are several ways readers provide this type of information to you. When readers use terms like *cozy, hard-boiled, noir,* or even *dark* in describing the types of mysteries they enjoy, they are giving you strong hints as to how much graphic violence they find acceptable. To understand how these terms play into the mystery readers' advisory interview, let's take a moment and discuss the use of *cozy, hard-boiled,* and *noir* when applied to a mystery.

COZY VERSUS HARD-BOILED: HOW READERS DEFINE THEIR TOLERANCE OF VIOLENCE IN THE GENRE

The term *cozy* was first traced to a mystery review published in 1958 and has gradually come to define a certain type of mystery (Herbert 1999, 97). Used by itself, *cozy* does not really represent a subgenre of its own. After all, cozy mysteries can be found in any number of mystery subgenres. When applied to a mystery, the term *cozy* has come to mean certain things for many readers. Most importantly, in a cozy mystery, the murder either takes place offstage or is handled in such a way that the reader does not receive graphic details about the crime. Violence is kept to a minimum in the cozy; these mysteries have a gentle atmosphere and a sense of civilized refinement. In many cozies, the murder takes place in a closed environment such as a country house, a small town, or an office. Most of the characters in a cozy either know one another or have some type of connection to each other. Psychopathic serial killers do not stalk victims in a cozy, and Patricia Cornwell has yet to write a cozy mystery. Murder disrupts the sense of order that prevails in a cozy world and only by solving the crime can order be restored. This sense that things have returned to normal and that order has been restored is very important to cozy readers.

Simply using the word *cozy* to describe a mystery can be confusing, especially because it can mean slightly different things to different readers. For some readers, the term *cozy* conjures up images of a small English village in which a spinster sleuths her way through crimes. These readers might be surprised when a readers' advisor offers them a series such as Diane Mott Davidson's Goldy Bear mysteries, featuring the Colorado catering sleuth, even though Davidson's books share a number of similar cozy qualities with the quintessential English village cozy. Other mystery readers sometimes use *cozy* to mean a traditional type of mystery, like those written by Elizabeth Daly, Ngaio Marsh, and Patricia Wentworth. In fact, many of the classic British authors of the 1920s and 1930s wrote mysteries that share characteristics with today's contemporary cozy mysteries. This is why it is important to clarify with the reader what *cozy* means to him or her.

It should be no surprise that most cozies come from the amateur sleuth subgenre, as many of these characteristics are already present in mysteries featuring an amateur sleuth, but there are cozies in other mystery subgenres, too. Both M. C. Beaton and Rhys Bowen write wonderfully cozy police procedural series. Carola Dunn as well as K. K. Beck write cozy historicals. When a reader mentions that she enjoys a good cozy mystery, she is, in effect, telling you something about how much violence she prefers in her mysteries. What she is not saying is that she prefers one specific subgenre of mysteries.

HARD-BOILED, SOFT-BOILED: WHAT DO EGGS HAVE TO DO WITH MYSTERIES?

Although some mystery readers relish a good cozy mystery, others want us to recommend a good hard-boiled detective novel. Once again the readers, by using these descriptors, may be giving you a clue as to how much violence they enjoy in their choice of a mystery.

Just as *cozy* has often come to signify the amateur sleuth subgenre for some readers, *hard-boiled* is most often used in reference to the private investigator subgenre of mysteries. The protagonist in a hard-boiled mystery is usually a tough loner, someone who is at odds with the outside world. This is an immediate contrast to the cozy sleuth, who is tied into a community and works with a close-knit circle of family, friends, and acquaintances. Most hard-boiled mysteries have a large urban setting, and there is an attempt to give the reader a realistically gritty look at murder. Corruption and violence are a part of the hard-boiled sleuth's world. In the best hard-boiled detective books, action and violence are an integral part of the plot, but they are never used as a shortcut for character development. Just as some mystery readers love the tone and atmosphere of a good cozy, others delight in the special appeal of the hard-boiled world.

Some of the classic private eye novelists have hard-boiled sleuths. Raymond Chandler, Dashiell Hammett, and Mickey Spillane in many ways shaped this type of mystery. With the arrival of women mystery writers such as Sue Grafton and Marcia Muller on the private eye scene, a new term was needed to qualify their private detectives. Thus, *soft-boiled* came into use to define mysteries, primarily private detective subgenre mysteries, that shared some characteristics with their classic counterparts but also softened the amount and level of graphic language and violence in their plots.

In addition to the use of *soft-boiled* and *hard-boiled* to describe mysteries, you may also encounter the term *noir* applied to mysteries. Some consider noir to be a type of hard-boiled fiction. The two do share similar characteristics, with perhaps the most important being an acceptance of violence, graphic language, and occasionally sex in a book's plot. Noir mysteries, however, often do not feature a private investigator as the protagonist. Classic examples of noir fiction include many of James M. Cain's novels, as well as Cornell Woolrich's books. Noir fiction does differ from many hard-boiled mysteries in that there is a general air of bleakness and despair. Even if hard-boiled detectives live in an unjust world, the reader can at least expect some form of justice to prevail in the end, but this is not always the case with noir fiction. Noir is all about mood and atmosphere, and it can tell you a lot about mystery readers' tastes if they say they enjoy this type of book.

When mystery readers use the terms *soft-boiled* and *hard-boiled* in describing their choice of reading, they are prompting you as to their comfort level in regard to violence and graphic language. A reader who loves Grafton's Kinsey Millhone may enjoy other soft-boiled private detective novels by authors such as Sarah Andrews, Martha Lawrence, Nevada Barr, and Doug Allyn, but the same reader might reject a hard-boiled series by an author such as Dennis Lehane. Just as there are those who prefer their eggs fixed in different ways, there are readers who want different levels of violence in their mystery fiction, and part of the mystery readers' advisory interview is determining how much violence readers are comfortable with in their mysteries.

CHARACTER, PLOT, A LITTLE OF BOTH; OR, WHAT DO READERS WANT?

Another important topic that should be explored as a reader discusses his or her likes and dislikes of mystery fiction is whether the reader prefers a character-driven story or a plot-driven story. Many mysteries can be divided into these two categories. Character-driven mysteries focus on the story's protagonist; plot-driven mysteries center more on the solving of the book's crime.

Perhaps the most extreme examples of plot-driven mysteries can be found among those books published in the first golden age of mystery fiction. In some of these books, readers were given a puzzle to solve, and everything from train schedules to floor plans had to be carefully scrutinized if they were to have any hope of solving the book's crime before the detective did. Conversely, extreme examples of character-driven mysteries can sometimes be located amidst the crop of mysteries published in the last decade. Some contemporary mystery authors devote so much space in their books to cataloging their protagonists' likes, dislikes, lifestyles, and circle of acquaintances that the mystery itself gets lost in all these personal details.

Most mysteries fall somewhere in between these two ends of the spectrum. The very best mysteries balance the twin demands of creating a compelling cast of characters with the challenge of working out an intriguing and puzzling mystery. Some readers do have a preference, though, and it pays to listen to their examples of authors they enjoy. If more-contemporary mystery writers are mentioned as favorites, the reader may prefer a mystery that is more character driven; if the reader loves classic mystery writers such as Rex Stout or Agatha Christie, a plot-driven mystery might be more his or her cup of reading tea. This is not to say that all classic mystery writers ignored character development in favor of plot but rather that the focus may have been more on developing the story than on spotlighting the sleuth.

Not only do some readers have a preference between plot-driven and character-driven mysteries, but there are also readers who favor certain types of characters over others. For example, some readers love Janet Evanovich's main character, bounty hunter Stephanie Plum, and find Stephanie to be earthy, sexy, and funny—just what they are looking for in a sleuth. Other readers might not appreciate Stephanie's charms and instead find her to be too loud, too vulgar, or too crude for their tastes. Likewise, some mystery readers adore Nancy Atherton's Aunt Dimity series for its cozy sweetness, but others may find it too twee for words. Sometimes the type of character that a mystery is structured around can be as important to the reader as the subgenre from which it comes.

GENDER, CONTENT, AND THE MYSTERY READER

Interestingly enough, gender can play a role in how some readers choose a book to read. More so than in other fiction genres, some mystery readers can and do tell us that they "prefer mysteries written by women or featuring female protagonists." Conversely, there are men who will not touch a book written by a female author. The gender of the author or the sleuth is one factor these readers use to determine what they will read. Perhaps the first time this type of split by gender occurs is with young mystery readers. How many boys will voluntarily pick up a Nancy Drew or Judy Bolton mystery?

This type of split by gender can be a bit perplexing at first to those of us who do not select our reading material by the author's or protagonist's gender, but it is something that can come up when you are doing a mystery readers' advisory interview. Fortunately, there are any number of excellent reference sources, including Willetta Heising's *Detecting Men* and *Detecting Women* series, that make finding mysteries with these qualifiers a breeze.

One danger we readers' advisors must be alert for is stereotyping readers. A sweet, grandmotherly little old lady comes to the desk and asks for a good mystery. Immediately we think of authors like Charlotte MacLeod or Virginia Rich; in reality, however, this reader wants the new John Sandford. "Certainly that man looking through a copy of the bestseller list wants the latest Grisham or Clancy," we think to ourselves, but to our surprise, we discover he wants to reserve the latest Diane Mott Davidson mystery. It can take a while to dismantle the preconceived notions we have about readers. The first step is really listening to the reader describe the types of mysteries he or she enjoys and not trying to second-guess the reader.

Occasionally you will find a mystery fan who reads for a certain theme. Nothing else matters as much to this type of reader than that the book be structured around certain plot elements. For example, some mystery readers love art mysteries, religious mysteries, culinary mysteries, or pet mysteries. Other elements, such as the subgenre, matter less to these readers than having certain key elements present in the story. Luckily, there are several mystery reference books, online sites, and at least one mystery periodical, *Mystery Readers Journal,* that can help locate mysteries centered on a certain theme, thus keeping this type of mystery reader happy.

I WANT ANOTHER ONE JUST LIKE . . . : THE APPEAL OF A SERIES

The question of series is yet one more thing you must keep in mind as you chat with readers about what type of mystery they enjoy. Series are an important part of the mystery genre, and they have certain elements that appeal to many readers (as well as publishers and authors). Some readers love discovering a new mystery series. After all, it means if they like the first book they read in the series, they have many more to enjoy. Other readers may be less enamored with the appeal of a series.

Mystery series not only introduce a whole raft of questions into your readers' advisory interview, but also present some new challenges. Some readers insist on starting a series at the beginning, feeling that picking up a book in the middle of a mystery series is like entering into a conversation that began before the reader arrived. This is one point you will need to clarify in the readers' advisory interview. In some cases, even if the reader does not care, the series is best read in order. For example, a reader who starts Dana Stabenow's Kate Shugak series with *Hunter's Moon,* the ninth book in the series, will discover that this book contains a dramatic plot development that changes everything. Reading the earlier books in this series might be less satisfying if the reader knows what is going to happen to characters later on.

In other series, an author develops a character over a range of books. At the end of Janet Evanovich's *High Five,* the title character, Stephanie Plum, finally hooks up romantically with one of the two men pursuing her, but readers do not discover the identity of this man until the opening chapter of *Hot Six.* In this case, most readers, if given the choice, will want to start Stephanie's adventures in bounty hunting at the beginning of the series, with *One for the Money.*

In other series, such as the John Putnam Thatcher mysteries, written by Emma Lathen, books can be read and enjoyed in any order because the series sleuth does not change significantly from book to book. The focus in this series is on the individual business settings for each book and the tightly constructed plots rather than the life of the detective. Many readers do not discover Agatha Christie's immortal detective Hercule Poirot in his first case, *The Mysterious Affair at Styles,* and this is fine, because the Poirot mysteries center on the puzzle aspect of the plot. With the exception of Poirot's final case, *Curtain,* in which Christie cunningly plays a final trick on readers, most of the Poirot mysteries can be read and enjoyed out of order. The best advice we can give when it comes to mystery series is, when in doubt, start the reader off with the first book your library has in a particular series.

Not only is dealing with mystery series a challenge to readers' advisors, but it can present some unique difficulties to the authors themselves. After all, how do you introduce regular series characters in your latest title to a reader who is just beginning your books without at the same time boring other readers who have been with you from the start? How do you keep a series fresh and original after the fifth, the tenth, even the twentieth book? Despite all the challenges writing a series presents, there are good reasons why mystery authors and publishers love series. For authors it can provide the opportunity to develop and expand a character over a period of time and to really explore all of their protagonist's traits, desires, and foibles. Publishers also love mystery series. They are easy to package and market, and there is the implied guarantee that each new title in a series is presold to a certain number of readers who are already fans of the author's work.

A successful series also presents both authors and publishers with the opportunity to build a brand-name type of recognition for their books. Just think of all those people who ask for the "alphabet books" (Sue Grafton's P.I. Kinsey Millhone series) or "those horse mysteries" (by Dick Francis).

Series are so popular with publishers that they are more than eager to keep a successful series going, even if the author dies and cannot provide them with more material. This was the case with the English village mysteries featuring Miss Seeton, which were originally written by Heron Carvic. After his death, James Melville took over the series, writing as Hampton Charles. Later, Sarah J. Mason picked up the series as Hamilton Crane, writing some fourteen books featuring the spinster sleuth. In this instance, the series successfully kept the cozy flavor of the books written by the original author. Perhaps that is helped by the pseudonyms assumed by Melville and Mason, which have the same initials as Heron Carvic and manage to convey that "British" feeling.

Series have become such an ingrained part of the mystery genre that there is even an annual "Mystery Series" week, which has been celebrated since 1998 and even has its own website (http://www.mysteryseriesweek.com) and pocket calendar. Mystery series are here to stay. They are popular with readers, beloved by publishers, embraced by many authors, and they can play an important part in the mystery readers' advisory interview.

AN AUTHOR BY ANY OTHER NAME

For any number of reasons, some mystery authors write, or may have written, under more than one name. Knowing this can sometimes play an important role in the readers' advisory interview.

One reason for authors to adopt a pseudonym stems from the number of books they may write within a particular time frame. Some mystery readers harbor the belief that if an individual author writes more than one or two books per year, these books must in some way be inferior, because the author appears to be churning out books while other authors sweat and labor for months or years over one single novel. This explains why in the past an author like John Creasey (who would seem to hold the record for mystery authors with pseudonyms, having written more than 560 novels under twenty different names) would choose several different pen names to present the illusion that more than one writer was actually responsible for all his work. Even today the misperception persists that the amount of time spent writing a book is directly proportional to the quality of the writing and how good the book is. An author who directly contradicts this assumption is the prolific P. C. Doherty, who has published more than thirty-five books to date. Doherty is the real author behind at least five different excellent historical mystery series, all written with different pseudonyms and all equally well written.

A few authors may need to use a pen name to keep their own identity private. Perhaps the best example of this is university professor Carolyn G. Heilbrun, who chose to write mysteries under the name Amanda Cross (Heising 2000). The tenor of the times and the views of her professional colleagues forced Heilbrun to hide from them the fact that she wrote (gasp!) popular fiction.

Other authors may choose to write under a pseudonym because they write different types of books. Using a different name is one way of clueing in readers that the books will be dissimilar. Author Barbara Mertz, who writes books about ancient Egypt under her own name, chooses to write under two different pseudonyms, Elizabeth Peters and Barbara Michaels, and has done so for more than thirty years. Readers can detect some subtle differences in the two "author" styles in that the Peters's books tend to have a stronger mystery component while the Michaels's books might be better identified as suspense with a strong romantic element. This is not to say that some mystery readers will not enjoy the books by Michaels as much as the books by Peters. In fact, many do enjoy both, and a knowledgeable readers' advisor will offer both authors to readers, with the above caveat.

A pseudonym can also be a way for two mystery authors to write under one name. When Susan Wittig Albert, author of the contemporary amateur sleuth series featuring China Bayles, began writing historical mysteries with her husband Bill Paige, they chose to use the name Robin Paige. Sisters Pamela O'Shaughnessy and Mary O'Shaughnessy write legal thrillers together under the name Perri O'Shaughnessy. Gail Frazer and Mary Pulver Kuhfeld wrote the first six of their historical Dame Frevisse series under the name Margaret Frazer. Now, Gail is continuing with the series on her own, still as Margaret Frazer. Mary herself is no stranger to pseudonyms. As Monica Ferris, she writes a cozy series featuring the owner of a needlework store (*Crewel World,* 1999), and as Mary Monica Pulver, she has written a series of police procedural mysteries, beginning with *Murder at the War* (1982; rereleased in 1991 as *Knight Fall*).

Publishers can also be a force propelling authors to use a pseudonym, with one example of this being the classic children's mystery series featuring Nancy Drew and the Hardy Boys. There was never really a Carolyn Keene or a Franklin Dixon. These were just names dreamed up by the Stratemeyer Syndicate, created by Edward L. Stratemeyer. In reality, a number of different authors wrote and continue to write these familiar mystery series.

Authors can also adopt a pseudonym as a means of protecting themselves against the ever-changing publishing world. With the rise of the supersized chain bookstores and increasing use of computerized inventory and sales records, authors have a limited window of time in which to prove themselves. If a particular bookstore orders a certain number of copies of an author's first mystery and fails to sell all of them, the bookstore may choose to order fewer copies of the author's next book. This will in turn further depress sales and may result in the author being permanently dropped by his publisher. Thus, some authors will find they need to reinvent themselves, complete with a new name, in order to start over in the mystery world. There is at least one instance in which this was done so successfully that a mystery was nominated for best first mystery category of the Edgars, only to later be dropped from the list of finalists after it came out that the book was the work of an established mystery author who had adopted a pseudonym.

Fortunately, there are a number of excellent resources to turn to when it comes to sleuthing out mystery pseudonyms. *Detecting Men* and *Detecting Women* both do an excellent job at providing connections between authors and their various names, as do *Crime Fiction II* (Hubin

1994) and *Silk Stalkings: More Women Write of Murder* (Nichols and Thompson 1998).

When providing readers' advisory, remember that it's an art, not a science. As with anything else—riding a bike, working a crossword puzzle, and yes, even reading a book—the more you do it, the better you get. Even when a particular suggestion is not a hit with a reader, don't be discouraged. A 100 percent success rate in readers' advisory just isn't going to happen because of the variety of readers and their myriad reading preferences and tastes. The true satisfaction in readers' advisory work comes from knowing that readers are comfortable sharing their love of books with you and find your library to be a place where people are willing to listen and talk with them about mysteries.

5

Resources: It's Who, Not What, You Know

With more than 1,000 mysteries being released each year, in addition to the wealth of classic mystery titles sitting on the shelves of our libraries, most of us find it difficult, if not impossible, to keep up with all the books this genre spawns. If, when suggesting titles to readers, we are forced to rely solely on those books we ourselves have read, many of us would run out of choices before our readers came back for seconds. Fortunately, there are other resources such as periodicals, reference books, and websites that can help us keep on top of our game.

These resources are the secret weapons readers' advisors can use in staying current with mystery fiction. Before we plunge into the many possible ways to acquire more knowledge about the mystery genre, we first need to clarify an important point about readers' advisory work that applies to all fiction genres. Readers' advisory service involves proposing titles that readers might like, offering them authors that may appeal to their particular reading interests, and giving them ideas as to future books they might want to explore. It is not possible to guarantee that a particular book will definitely appeal to a reader at any given point in time. There are just too many variables.

If you change the focus of your readers' advisory interview so that you are providing suggestions, ideas, and possibilities for the reader, you will open up a broader pool of authors and titles from which you can draw upon. Being a good readers' advisor does not mean that you must personally have read, and enjoyed, every title you offer to a reader. This is an impossible goal. Being a good readers' advisor simply means knowing enough about a particular mystery, whether it is information garnered from book reviews, a website, a reference source, or even another reader, that you can reasonably expect that an individual mystery reader might be interested in it. This is how familiarity with mystery periodicals, a good collection of reference books, and a list of favorite websites can be of immense help. In effect, you are giving yourself more material to work with and your reader more potential choices.

MYSTERY MAGAZINES

Most of us are familiar with the traditional sources for reviews of mysteries, such as *Booklist, Library Journal,* and *Publishers Weekly.* These are important sources for keeping up with what is being published and selecting titles for your library's collection. However, if these are the only periodicals you are looking at to get information about mystery fiction, you are missing out on a wide assortment of authors and titles.

Genre-specific mystery magazines have been around almost as long as mysteries themselves. Many of these magazines, especially the early periodicals like *Black Mask,* were dedicated to publishing original mystery short stories and novellas. Perhaps the first mystery magazine that provided a showcase for the genre in its entirety was the *Armchair Detective.* Founded by Allen J. Hubin in 1967, the *Armchair Detective* opened to readers a whole world of mysteries. Issues included reviews of current mystery titles, interviews with contemporary mystery writers, and articles on the history of the genre and classic mystery authors. Mystery readers gobbled this periodical up because there is nothing fans like more than finding someone who shares their interests. For more than thirty years, the *Armchair Detective* offered a way for mystery readers, writers, publishers, and critics to share their common love of the genre.

Unfortunately, the *Armchair Detective* ceased publication in 1997. Fortunately, there are other mystery periodicals available, ranging from scholarly to frothy in tone, to help fill this void. Subscribing to one or more mystery periodicals is an easy way to keep up with the genre, especially for those of us who are pressed for time. Magazines like *Mystery News, Deadly Pleasures,* and the *Drood Review of Mystery* provide thoughtful criticism and reviews of current mystery books, offer articles on past and present crime and mystery writers, and include information about recent award winners and mystery conferences.

Each of these mystery periodicals has its own unique features and flavor. For the past few years, the *Drood Review* has provided an annual article focusing on the year's Edgar Award winners with comments on each of the nominated books by the periodical's critics. Each issue of *Deadly Pleasures* includes a section called "Reviewed to Death," in which a variety of that magazine's reviewers take a look at the same mystery book and offer their opinions. Reading through all of their comments clearly demonstrates how individual readers can react differently to the same book. *Mystery News* is an excellent source for in-depth articles and profiles on contemporary crime and mystery writers. Each of these magazines also includes information on forthcoming mystery titles as well as insightful reviews on a wide range of current mystery books.

In addition to periodicals that cover the entire mystery genre, there are numerous magazines and newsletters devoted to a particular niche of mystery fiction. Does your library have patrons who clamor for more cozy mysteries? Subscribe to *Murder Most Cozy,* a newsletter dedicated to everything cozy. It includes author interviews, information on new and forthcoming cozy mysteries, and a special crimeless cozy section (which is also a valuable resource when it comes to locating titles for those readers who enjoy gentle reads).

Mystery Readers Journal: The Journal of Mystery Readers International (MRJ) is priceless when it comes to locating mysteries centered on a specific theme. Published quarterly, *MRJ* has devoted entire issues to such topics as gardening mysteries, art mysteries, mysteries set in France, and academic mysteries. Each issue provides a nice mix of articles about authors and articles written by mystery writers themselves. Because *MRJ* does not focus solely on just current mystery titles, it can also be an excellent source for learning more about classic mystery authors.

Book publishers also offer their own version of mystery newsletters. Simon and Schuster and Scribner publish *Inner Sanctum,* a newsletter of crime and mystery fiction. The spring 2001 issue featured interviews with authors Jan Burke, John Dunning, and Kathy Reichs, among others, in addition to information on forthcoming mysteries from this publisher. For years St. Martin's Press mailed out an excellent monthly newsletter, *Murder at the Flatiron,* with details about its forthcoming mystery titles as well as a column from its "mysterious" editor. Now that St. Martin's Press has established a website, the monthly newsletter has switched to e-mail format. Just subscribe at the website to receive the electronic *Murder at the Flatiron* as well as updates to other links on the site.

Other websites also offer their e-mail-based newsletters and mystery updates. *January Magazine* has a special *Crime Fiction* newsletter with reviews of current mystery fiction and profiles of mystery authors—free for the asking. Even that venerable Web presence Amazon.com offers you the opportunity to sign up for current mystery title updates that then arrive like clockwork in your e-mail box.

Many authors publish and distribute newsletters, often in connection with their own websites. These can be a valuable resource for readers' advisory staff. One example of this is mystery writer Susan Wittig Albert's free e-mail newsletter. In addition to tidbits about herbs and gardening, you will also learn the latest on her China Bayles series as well as the historical mysteries she writes with her husband, Bill, under the name Robin Paige.

MPM—a quarterly bulletin on the doings and undoings of mystery writer Barbara Mertz/Elizabeth Peters/Barbara Michaels—has been published for years. It offers fans of this author a way to keep current on the latest mystery by their favorite author and inside details on the writing process, the author's characters, and other information. Getting a copy of this print newsletter is as easy as requesting to be added to the mailing list.

Whether it's subscribing to a traditional mystery magazine like *Mystery News* or joining an e-mail newsletter like *Crime Fiction,* there are a number of ways mystery readers' advisors can stay up-to-date with the genre with a minimum of muss and fuss. *See* appendix C, "Genre Resources," page 180, for more information on mystery magazines.

MYSTERY REFERENCE SOURCES

Sadly, there is no single, all-purpose, multiuse, suitable-for-every-question mystery reference source. This is the reason why a good mystery readers' advisory reference collection should contain a number of different titles, each varying in focus and type of information included. Some reference books, such as *By a Woman's Hand,* can be grabbed and used in the midst of a readers' advisory interview, but other titles, such as *Mystery and Suspense Writers,* are better suited for a time when the readers' advisor can sit down and read through a section in an effort to gain a better understanding of an author's place in the genre or the characteristics of a subgenre. A diverse selection of mystery reference sources is one of the best ways staff can learn more about the genre.

Most libraries will want to keep a number of mystery readers' advisory resources handy to their reference desks, because nothing breaks the flow of a readers' advisory interview more than having to search for a reference book you need. However, don't make the mistake of thinking these mystery reference sources are only useful to those of us doing the readers' advisory interview. Consider purchasing a few of the more reasonably priced mystery guides for your circulating collection as well. You may be surprised at how many readers will enjoy being able to take these books home, where they can use them to come up with their own lists of new authors and titles to try.

As you build up your mystery readers' advisory reference collection, it can be quite tempting to discard an old copy when a new edition of a favorite source arrives. When it comes to weeding your mystery readers' advisory sources, however, the watchword is *caution.* Some newer editions do not include all previous material when they are revised or updated. A good example is *Detecting Women,* by Willetta L. Heising. The latest, third edition notes that 225 new authors have been added. Quite a number of authors have also been dropped, however, because of the death of the author or for other considerations. The earlier editions of *Detecting Women* are the sources for information on books by these authors. Hold on to them. Even if you don't have room in your ready-reference collection, space should be found for these still valuable sources. Appendix C, page 182, lists mystery reference books.

MYSTERY WEBSITES

The World Wide Web is becoming increasingly popular with readers' advisors as they try to meet the challenge of matching books with readers. Websites do have some unique advantages over their print reference counterparts. They can be updated more frequently than print sources. A mystery website can be used by a potentially unlimited number of users in more than one location. Some websites even have the capability of letting readers interact with their favorite authors or share their opinions with other fans of the genre. When it comes to building a mystery reference collection, most mystery readers' advisors will want to bookmark their preferred websites to use along with their favorite print resources.

How will you know whether to head for a computer or the reference stacks first? It usually depends on the specific nature of the question you are working on. Do you need a list of the most recent Edgar Award winners? A website is probably going to give you this information. Want to know something about a forthcoming mystery book by St. Martin's Press? Head over to its website to get the gist and see when the book will hit the bookstores. Need background information on a mystery author? Depending on the author and how recently his or her work was published, you may have better luck finding something about the author on the Web, though even classic mystery authors such as Agatha Christie and Dorothy Sayers have some terrific websites devoted to them.

In some cases the line between traditional print reference sources and the Web is blurring. One example of this is Gale's *What Do I Read Next?* series, which is available both in book form and as a Web-based product. The mystery section is the same in both versions of this product, but libraries can now choose the format that works best for them and their readers.

Discussion groups, a close counterpart to websites, can be an excellent way of getting to know more about a subject or keeping up with current trends. Just look at the number of librarians who subscribe to discussion groups like PUBLIB and ALSC. There are groups dedicated to specific mystery subgenres as well as individual authors, but the one discussion group that comes the closest to covering the depth and range of the mystery genre is DorothyL. Created by a group of female librarians at a professional meeting in 1991, DorothyL is currently sent out either in a daily digest format or as individual messages to its subscribers. Topics covered include reviews and opinions of current and past mystery fiction, movies, television shows, and authors. Discussions of mystery awards, mystery bookstores, and the process of mystery writing also come up on the site. Archives of previous digests are also available on the Web. Like any discussion group, there can be some chaff among the wheat, but DorothyL provides mystery readers' advisors with a wonderful opportunity to learn more about the writers and books in this genre.

A wealth of information about the mystery genre is available on the Web, and many readers' advisory staff will want to share their favorite sites with their patrons, either by creating links on a library's catalog or by adding website addresses to your printed book lists. But it pays to remember that anyone with a computer and a modem can publish something on the Web. Evaluate your mystery reference websites as carefully as you select your reference books. *See* appendix C, page 186, for a list of excellent websites.

MYSTERY ASSOCIATIONS AND AWARDS

There are a number of different associations and groups dedicated to sharing their love of the mystery genre. Some groups embrace the total mystery experience; others focus on a particular niche of the genre. Becoming aware of these different associations, knowing more about their goals and objectives, and perhaps even joining a group or two can be another excellent way of increasing your own knowledge of the genre.

Sisters in Crime was founded in 1986 by a small group of female mystery writers, including Sara Paretsky, who were concerned that their books were not receiving the same amount of press attention as their male counterparts. From this initial meeting, a national association of authors, booksellers, editors, agents, librarians, critics, teachers, and readers was born to "combat discrimination against women in the mystery field, educate publishers and the general public as to inequities in the treatment of female authors, raise awareness of their contribution to the field, and promote the professional advancement of women who write mysteries." Sisters in Crime has approximately 3,000 members throughout the world, as well as local chapters in many areas of the United States. Sisters in Crime is very librarian friendly, and members can usually be found at ALA's national conferences, either at the Sisters in Crime booth at the exhibits area or through the mystery author breakfast the association sponsors at the Annual Conference. Men are welcome to become members of Sisters in Crime if they can commit to the organization's goals and purposes. Joining Sisters in Crime is an easy way to get to know mystery authors as well as learn more about the genre itself.

Mystery Writers of America is a "nonprofit professional organization of mystery and crime writers in all categories: fiction, including adult novels, short stories, and YA and juvenile fiction; screenplays, staged plays, radio plays, and TV; and nonfiction, including fact crime and critical/biographical work." Inspired by British crime and mystery writers who had been meeting regularly, Mystery Writers of America was incorporated in 1945, and among its founding members were such writers as Rex Stout, Ellery Queen, and Erle Stanley Gardner. Members of Mystery Writers of America include mystery and crime writers as well as editors, publishers, and other industry professionals. Librarians can join Mystery Writers of America through its associate membership category. Mystery Writers of America is perhaps best known to librarians for its annual mystery-writing awards, the Edgars.

Private Eye Writers (PWA) of America is a group of writers, fans, and publishing professionals devoted to the appreciation and promotion of private eye mysteries. It was founded in 1982 by Robert J. Randisi, who has also served as president. Other well-known authors have served as PWA president, including Bill Pronzini, Sue Grafton, Jeremiah Healy, and Sara Paretsky. The associate level membership is one in which librarians who love P.I. mysteries will be most interested. Each year Private Eye Writers of America awards the Shamus Awards in various categories.

Known for its publication *Mystery Readers Journal: The Journal of Mystery Readers International,* Mystery Readers International promotes itself as "the largest mystery fan/reader organization in the world." Membership is open to all readers, fans, critics, editors, publishers, and writers of mysteries. Founded by Janet A. Rudolph, the organization has members in all fifty of the United States and twenty-two foreign countries. There are local chapters of this organization in different parts of the country, and members are eligible to vote for the group's annual Macavity Awards.

Founded by British mystery writer John Creasey in 1953, the Crime Writers Association can be considered Great Britain's counterpart to the Mystery Writers of America. Representing "writers of crime fiction and nonfiction," the Crime Writers Association has about 400 members, including many famous British mystery writers, as well as a few American writers. The Crime Writers Association offers different categories of membership and annually awards a series of Dagger Awards for the best crime and mystery books in various categories.

Who Is Edgar and Why Is Someone Giving Him an Award?

Like all the other fiction genres, mystery fiction likes to recognize its best and brightest in the form of a number of different awards. Many mystery awards are connected to one of the genre's associations or fan groups. Basically, there are two different kinds of mystery awards: fan and professional. Knowing a bit more about some of these awards and how they are selected can help you with readers' advisory questions and mystery collection development needs.

Agatha Awards, named after Agatha Christie, honor "traditional" mysteries and are given out in four categories: Best Novel, Best First Mystery, Best Short Story, and Best Non-Fiction. First given in 1988, this award is a fan-generated one in which registrants for the annual Malice Domestic convention receive ballots to nominate their choices for each category. The Agatha Awards Committee tallies these ballots, and a short list of final nominees (five from each category) is drawn up. These final nominees are voted upon by conference registrants, and the awards are given out at the Malice Domestic conference.

Anthony Awards are named after the renowned mystery critic Anthony Boucher and have been given out at the annual Bouchercon mystery conference since 1985. Anthony Awards are another fan-generated award in which the registrants for Bouchercon nominate their choices for categories such as Best Novel, Best First Novel, Best Paperback Original, Best Short Story, and Best Critical Nonfiction. Those attending the Bouchercon then vote on the final list of nominees.

Arthur Ellis Awards, gifted with the working name of Canada's hangman, have been given since 1984 to Canadian crime and mystery writers by the Crime Writers of Canada. Categories include Best Novel, Best True Crime, Best First Novel, Best Short Story, and Best Juvenile Mystery.

Dagger Awards are bestowed by the Crime Writers Association, a British mystery writers association. The Diamond Dagger is awarded to a mystery writer in recognition of a lifetime's achievements in crime writing, a Gold Dagger is presented to the best mystery or crime novel, and a Silver Dagger is awarded to the runner-up. Daggers are also given out to the Best Non-Fiction book and Short Story. The John Creasey Memorial Dagger is awarded to the Best First Mystery. The Ellis Peters Historical Dagger is a recent addition and is given out to the Best

Historical Mystery. Submission for the Dagger Awards is by publishers only, and the awards are judged either by a panel of newspaper and magazine critics or experts in the field.

The Dilys Award, named after mystery bookseller Dilys Winn, has been given annually since 1992 by members of the Independent Mystery Booksellers Association for the new mystery title "they most enjoyed selling."

Edgar Awards, named after Edgar Allen Poe, were first presented in 1946 by the Mystery Writers of America. Currently, awards are given for Best Novel, Best First Novel, Best Paperback Original, Best Critical/ Biographical Work, Best Fact Crime, Best Short Story, Best Children's Mystery, and Best Young Adult Mystery. Edgars are also awarded in the categories of television, movies, and plays. Submission for the Edgar Awards is by publishers only, and each award is judged by a committee composed of five members of the Mystery Writers of America.

The Hammett Award is presented to a U.S. or Canadian crime writer for a work of literary excellence in the field of crime writing by the North American Branch of the International Association of Crime Writers, who uses a trio of independent judges to select the winner. The Hammett is named in honor of that classic mystery author Dashiell Hammett and has been given since 1996.

Macavity Awards have been given since 1987 by the members of Mystery Readers International, who nominate their favorite titles and then vote on the final list. Four Macavity Awards are given out in the categories of Best Mystery Novel, Best First Mystery Novel, Best Nonfiction, and Best Mystery Short Story. The award derives its name from T. S. Eliot's "mystery cat" in his book *Old Possum's Book of Practical Cats.*

Ned Kelly Awards are given out by the Crime Writers Association of Australia in the categories of Best Australian Crime Novel, Best First Australian Crime Novel, and Best True Crime. "Neddies" have been awarded since 1996 and are named after a notorious Australian criminal.

Nero Wolfe Awards are the product of a fan group, the Wolfe Pack, who dedicate themselves to the appreciation and study of Nero Wolfe. First awarded in 1979, the Nero Wolfe Award is given to one book that best reflects Rex Stout's type of mystery writing.

Shamus Awards are bestowed annually by the Private Eye Writers of America, whose members select the Best P.I. Novel, Best P.I.

Paperback Original, Best P.I. First Novel, Best P.I. Short Story, and the "Eye" Lifetime Achievement Award. The Shamus Awards have been given since 1982 and are named in honor of the lone private investigator, or shamus.

MYSTERY BOOKSTORES

Mystery bookstores are a librarian's best friend. If you are fortunate enough to live near an independent mystery bookstore, thank your lucky stars, for it can be a gold mine of useful readers' advisory information. Most mystery bookstores have the same goal as libraries offering readers' advisory services: they want to help match readers with books they may enjoy. Many mystery bookstores go about this in the same way libraries do by offering author programs, staff who can help suggest authors and titles to try, and newsletters and websites that showcase new and upcoming mystery books.

Attending an author program at a mystery bookstore can be both educational and fun. Hearing authors speak about their work or answer questions about their characters is an easy way for you to discover their appeal to other readers. For example, even if you are not a personal fan of hard-boiled mysteries, listening to an author like Dennis Lehane or George Pelecanos can give you insight as to the attraction his work has for other readers.

Many of the staff working at mystery bookstores are dedicated and knowledgeable readers of the genre. Don't care for cozy mysteries yourself? Find a bookstore staff member who does and ask for his or her favorite cozy titles. The next time patrons query you for this type of read, you can draw upon this information and tell them that although you yourself have not read a particular title, it is a favorite at this bookstore.

Mystery bookstore websites and newsletters are worth their weight in gold. Many mystery bookstores offer their own newsletters in both print and electronic formats. For example, the Poisoned Pen's *Booknews* is a veritable monthly feast of information on new and forthcoming mystery and crime novels. Learning about new and old mystery authors and books from the perspective of a knowledgeable, perceptive critic like Barbara Peters, Arizona's Poisoned Pen's owner, is worth the *Booknews*'s minimal subscription cost. Colorado's High Crimes Mystery Bookshop is another independent mystery bookstore with an excellent monthly newsletter, in this case, the *Purloined Letter.* The Partners in Crime mystery bookstore in New York has an exceptional website that offers author interviews, an ever-changing selection of "partner's picks" books, and a list of its own 100 best mysteries. These are just a few examples of the many opportunities mystery readers' advisory staff have when they get to know a mystery bookstore. Any time you can gain an additional viewpoint or opinion of a book, it will make you a better reader's advisor.

Need a list of mystery bookstores or want to know if there is one near you? The Independent Mystery Booksellers Association produces a directory of its members that provides names, addresses, website information—everything you need to get in touch with one of its member stores. The Independent Mystery Booksellers Association also has its own fabulous website with all of this information as well as a list of its own members' 100 favorite mystery books.

MYSTERY CONFERENCES

A mystery conference offers a wonderful opportunity to meet with authors, critics, and fans of this genre. Whether you want a relatively smaller conference experience, such as Malice Domestic, or the full-blown glory of Bouchercon, the genre's largest conference, there truly is something for everyone.

Bouchercon is the oldest as well as the largest of the mystery genre's conventions. Held in honor of mystery writer and influential critic William Anthony Parker White (who wrote under the name Anthony Boucher), Bouchercon is an annual event that draws thousands of fans, writers, publishers, critics, and booksellers together. The location of Bouchercon changes from year to year, and it can be quite overwhelming to attend your first Bouchercon. Think of Bouchercon as the American Library Association Annual Conference of the mystery world.

Malice Domestic, first held in 1989, celebrates "mysteries of manners," or those mysteries written in a traditional style, such as the works of Agatha Christie, in which there is an absence of graphic violence, language, and explicit sex. Malice Domestic is always held in the Washington, D.C., area, takes place in the spring, and registration is limited to a certain number.

Left Coast Crime, another of the smaller conferences, celebrates all types of mysteries, but the location of the conference is always held in a western state. If you have never attended a mystery conference, Left Coast Crime is an excellent choice. The number of fans attending is not overwhelming, and the time frame for the conference is manageable. Because all different types of mysteries are included in the programming, there is usually something for every mystery reader to enjoy.

In addition to these conferences, there are also conferences dedicated to the study and appreciation of individual mystery writers. The Dorothy Sayers Society offers an annual conference in Great Britain that focuses on this golden age mystery writer. John D. MacDonald has been the subject of several conferences held in Florida. Mystery bookstores themselves can host a small mystery conference, such as the Poisoned Pen's "Murder Goes . . ." Conferences, which have covered such topics as art mysteries and classic mysteries.

Don't feel overwhelmed by this plethora of mystery resources. The point of this chapter is to illustrate that you do not need to know everything about mystery fiction to be an effective readers' advisor. Through the wide range of genre resources, whether they are Web-based, traditional print sources, genre periodicals, or associations, you can expand your own base of knowledge about mystery fiction and become a more effective readers' advisor.

6

Collection Development

E ffective readers' advisory service does not take place in a vacuum. You can be the best readers' advisor in the world, but if you do not have the books you are suggesting for your patrons in your library's collection, you might just as well lock your doors. For some readers your collection will be their sole experience with readers' advisory service. For whatever reason, these readers will not ask for suggestions at a service desk but will instead choose their recreational reading by browsing through your library's stacks. If your collection does not have anything waiting to tempt them, they will walk away disappointed and empty-handed.

ASSESSING YOUR MYSTERY COLLECTION

Most of us think of collection development simply as the selection and acquisition of materials. However, cataloging and processing of those materials, in addition to weeding, are just as much a part of collection development as picking out books from review journals. But before you can do any of these activities, you first need to know your collection.

Successful collection development involves a plan and a vision for your library's holdings. The starting point of this process is known formally as collection assessment. By doing this you gain an idea of what your collection consists of and who its users are. Collection assessment can be done in a quick and cursory manner, sometimes known as impressionistic collection assessment, or take on a more structured and formal approach. Whichever method is used, collection assessment is essential to developing a quality mystery section.

The first step in assessing your mystery collection is to get out in the stacks and devote some uninterrupted time to studying your collection. Whether you spend an hour or two on one particular day or stretch the process out over several days or even weeks, it is important to actually experience the same environment that your patrons encounter when they go in search of a good book to read. Be sure to bring along something to record your observations. Take note of what authors you have, the condition of the books, what titles seem to be missing, and what titles have an inch-thick frosting of dust.

Comparing your mystery collection against standard "core lists" is one direction an assessment project can take. In addition to the better-known readers' advisory reference tools such as *Genreflecting, Fiction Catalog,* and *Sequels,* other mystery genre resources such as *Detecting Men* and *Detecting Women* can be used as checklists to determine what authors and titles are missing from your collection. Lists of award winners, such as the Edgars, the Agathas, or the Anthonys, are excellent tools that can also be used to evaluate what is available in your library.

If possible, involve other library staff in your assessment process. Frequently, your library's circulation staff and pages know which authors are popular simply because they see what is checking out and being reshelved on a regular basis. If there is time for a long-range assessment project, ask desk staff to keep track of mystery authors and titles they receive requests for, especially those that are not in your library's collection. If you have any library staff who are mystery readers themselves, solicit their thoughts and impressions on the state of your mystery collection. One benefit of involving other staff members in your collection assessment project is that they will become more aware of the mystery collection. They may even be more willing in the future to let you know when gaps crop up in the collection.

While you are assessing your mystery collection, it is essential to remember that collections are built for individual communities of readers.

There is no one standard group of mystery authors and titles that is going to be a perfect match for all libraries. Knowing what is popular with readers in your community is part of being a good collection development librarian as well as a good readers' advisor. In some communities, historical mysteries might fly off the shelves; in other libraries, readers cannot get enough hard-boiled private eye mysteries. Learning to recognize these patterns can help guide future purchasing decisions.

The ratio of mystery fiction to other genre fiction will vary from library to library. In some libraries, science fiction or romance fiction might be more popular than mysteries. This does not mean that a library in this situation can ignore purchasing mysteries. It does mean that this library might not devote as much of its fiction budget to mysteries as another library where mystery fiction is more popular.

The worst collection development trap to fall into is to think that one particular genre is not popular with readers in your community. This may lead you to neglect purchasing books of this type. Then, those readers who might be looking for this kind of book will find nothing of interest in your collection, which in turn reinforces your perceptions that no one in your community reads this genre. All public libraries need at least some books, classic and current titles, from every fiction genre, including mysteries. It is just the ratio of titles in a collection that will vary from library to library.

Assessing your mystery collection is not an ending point in and of itself. The assessment process should lead to something, whether it is the decision to "beef up" your mystery collection or give the collection a good weeding. With the recent knowledge you have gained about your mystery collection, the post-assessment period is also the perfect time to update or write a collection development policy. If your library already has a collection development policy, check to see whether fiction, including mysteries, is covered. If your library does not have a collection development policy, use the information you have gathered from your assessment to write one.

A mystery collection development policy does not have to be a long, labor-intensive effort. The policy itself can address such issues as the scope of the collection, how often the collection will be weeded, what factors will influence purchasing decisions, the number of copies of a particular title that will be purchased to satisfy a reserve list, and how gifts will be handled.

SELECTING MYSTERY FICTION

After assessing your mystery collection you are now ready for the fun job of ordering mysteries. Several factors will influence how you choose mysteries for your library—library type, budget, demand, and collection comprehensiveness. The first factor is to determine the type of library for which you are selecting. Choosing mystery fiction for a small branch is different from selecting mystery books for the main library in a system. A branch library may only need to have an assortment of the most popular mystery authors and titles, but the main library will need to have a broader collection that can be shared systemwide. Academic libraries can have totally different needs from their public counterparts. Instead of adding popular current mystery titles to satisfy recreational reading, some academic libraries may emphasize the selection of classic mystery authors and titles to fill curriculum needs.

Your library's budget for mystery fiction is the second factor affecting selection and collection development. No matter how many new mystery authors and titles you want to buy, in the end it all comes down to how much money you have to spend. Will your budget be used only for the purchase of current mystery fiction or does your library allocate funds for retrospective collection development as well? If you are selecting for multiple branches in a system, do you have an idea of how much money should be devoted to each branch's collection?

The popularity of mystery fiction with your community's readers will also guide the selection and collection development process. Some libraries will want to dedicate a good portion of their fiction budget to mysteries, but others may not need to commit as many resources to this genre. As stated before, the representation of different genres in your fiction collection is a matter of individual community tastes.

The current state of your mystery collection is yet another factor influencing the selection and collection development process in your library. If, after doing your assessment, you discover your collection has significant gaps, you will need to devote resources to bringing your mystery collection up to snuff. Having attractive-looking copies of classic mysteries in your collection can be as important to some readers as having the latest copy of a hot title is to others.

In many libraries, materials selection is done using review journals. Most of the standard library review sources, such as *Booklist, Library*

Journal, and *Publishers Weekly,* have a section devoted to mystery fiction and review mystery titles on a regular basis. Using these magazines is the first step in selecting titles for your mystery collection. However, you cannot rely solely on these tried-and-true selection periodicals if you want to build a dynamic mystery collection. The sheer number of books being published each year simply precludes any single review magazine from ever being able to cover all mysteries.

If you want a mystery collection that is the envy of libraries for miles around, you must supplement traditional library review journals with other sources. Start by looking at the periodicals your patrons use when they need ideas of what mysteries to read. Many readers are fans of the *New York Times Book Review*'s mystery column, written by Marilyn Stasio, whose wickedly sharp pen manages to convey the strengths and flaws of several current mysteries, each within a few paragraphs. Want to know why all your patrons are clamoring for Laura Van Wormer's *Jury Duty* or Brad Meltzer's *First Counsel?* Perhaps it's because they saw it in *People Weekly's* "Pages" section, which often drops a mystery title or two among its "picks." *Book: The Magazine for the Reading Life* is another excellent periodical popular with the general public that often has articles on mystery and crime writers in addition to book reviews. Local newspapers are frequently the first place readers hear about a mystery, so don't forget to check to see if your local paper has a regular book review section.

Now that you have an idea of what your patrons are looking at, pick one or more of the genre-specific periodicals mentioned in chapter 5, such as *Mystery News* or the *Drood Review of Mystery,* and add it to the selection journals you use. By including more reviews of paperback original mysteries, in addition to more mysteries published by smaller presses, these genre-specific periodicals will give you a better idea of the range of mysteries currently available.

Vendor catalogs, such as Baker and Taylor's *Paperclips* and Ingram's *Paperback Advance,* can also be valuable mystery selection tools. Both of these catalogs include many of the paperback original mysteries published for that month as well as those titles being reissued. In addition to their selection catalogs, some vendors can even help you save time by offering tailor-made collection development lists for certain subjects or by helping you set up a standing order plan for something like paperback mysteries.

Publisher catalogs are another effective and free way of keeping up with what is coming out in the mystery genre. Knowing which titles are going to be pushed by a publisher like Simon and Schuster or Random House will give you an idea of what mysteries are going to be the subject of a buzz months before they are reviewed or appear in a bookstore. An added readers' advisory benefit of perusing publishers' catalogs is that you can tip off your favorite patrons about forthcoming titles by their favorite authors.

SIGHTS AND SOUNDS OF MYSTERY

For many libraries, materials selection and collection development do not stop just with books. Media—audiocassettes, compact discs, and videos—are all part of some library's collections and must be selected on a regular basis. Fortunately, the mystery genre is equally at home in these formats as it is on the printed page. Mention Poirot or Miss Marple to some mystery fans and, instead of books, these admirers think of David Suchet's or Joan Hickson's letter-perfect performances in PBS's *Mystery!* productions (currently available on VHS and DVD). The latest Patricia Cornwell mystery your patrons are talking about? They didn't read the book; they heard it on cassette or compact disc while they were commuting. Developing or adding to a mystery media collection can be an excellent way to build your circulation statistics and please your mystery-loving patrons.

Those libraries that are starting their mystery media collections from scratch have some excellent resources to turn to. Reference books such as Otto Penzler's *101 Greatest Films of Mystery and Suspense* can provide a plethora of classic and contemporary mystery movies that a collection development librarian can then check for availability in VHS or DVD format. Many of PBS's beloved *Mystery!* productions are also available on VHS or DVD, as are a number of the original mystery movies shown on the A & E cable channel. Another method of coming up with some possibilities for your video collection is to go through the list of Edgar Awards presented for Best Motion Picture. Check on the availability of these titles and then use this list to build a terrific VHS or DVD collection. Even Amazon.com has continually updated sections devoted to mystery and suspense in both VHS and DVD formats that savvy collection development librarians can use as food for thought.

Audiocassettes and compact discs can also be an important part of your library's mystery collection. Just as there are some readers who eagerly await the next book in Elizabeth Peters's Amelia Peabody series, there are some listeners who wait just as anxiously for Recorded Books to bring out the same book on tape. Most libraries will want to purchase both abridged and unabridged audiocassettes for their mystery collections because patrons often have strong preferences for one format or the other. An increasing number of publishers, including trendsetter Random House, are also bringing out their books in compact disc format, which is perfect for those commuter mystery readers whose cars have disc players.

When you are selecting mystery titles for your audio collection, keep in mind that no one likes to listen to just part of a series any more than they want to read just a few titles by the same mystery author. If you have Lawrence Block's Bernie Rhodenbarr series or Nevada Barr's Anna Pigeon mysteries in audio, try to get all of the titles in these series for your collection.

Expanding the concept of your mystery collection to include both audio and video formats will prove to be a positive experience for both you and your patrons. Not only will your library enjoy the benefits of increased circulation statistics, but you will also receive grateful accolades from mystery fans themselves, who can now experience their favorite genre in an entirely new way.

NOT JUST NEW BUT OLD

Sometimes in the rush to add the latest hot thriller or popular true crime book to our collections, we forget about the classic mystery authors. As difficult as it might be for some of us to imagine, there are readers out there, both young and old, who have never had the joy of discovering mysteries by Agatha Christie, Rex Stout, or Ellery Queen. Part of collection development is seeing to it that your library has copies of books by these and other classic mystery authors.

This type of selection, often called retrospective collection development, needs to be done on a regular basis. When mystery books or other materials are lost, damaged, or stolen, they need to be replaced so that other readers can enjoy them. In a large library this process can be as time-consuming and demanding as the selection of new materials, so it is best to work out some type of plan for retrospective collection development in advance. One way of handling retrospective collection development if you have a large collection, or if you have a smaller collection but not much time to devote to it, is to break down your collection into manageable pieces. Choose authors from a certain part of the alphabet to concentrate on for one year. Or pick a few series by different mystery authors that you can then check for gaps.

In the last few years several small mystery publishers have sprung up that can help you with your retrospective collection development needs. Two of the best of this bunch of small presses are Rue Morgue Press and the Poisoned Pen Press. Based in Colorado, Rue Morgue Press was founded by mystery booksellers Tom Schantz and Enid Schantz as a way of bringing back into print mystery classics that had long since vanished from most bookstores and libraries. Just a few of the authors Rue Morgue is in the midst of reprinting include Joanna Cannan, Constance Little and Gwenyth Little, and Charlotte Murray Russell. Rue Morgue has even introduced classic mystery titles never before available in the United States, such as *Common or Garden Crime,* by Sheila Pim. This wonderfully cozy gardening mystery, originally published in Great Britain, is now making its first appearance in America, courtesy of this press.

Poisoned Pen Press, founded in 1996 by mystery bookseller Barbara Peters, her husband, Robert Rosenwald, and their daughter, Susan, has several missions. Bringing back into print "missing mysteries" is one of them. Mysteries such as *Penny Black,* by Susan Moody, and *Murder in C Major,* by Sara Hoskinson Frommer, have been attractively republished and can now be added to your library's collection once again, thanks to the hard work and efforts of this publisher.

British publisher Chivers Press also deserves the gratitude of mystery readers and librarians everywhere for its reprint series called Black Dagger Crime. This ongoing series, which began in 1987, resulted from a cooperative effort between the publisher and a subcommittee of the British Crime Writers Association to bring back into print outstanding examples of every type of detective stories. Just a few of the authors included in this reprint series are Joan Aiken, Christianna Brand,

Gwendoline Butler, Francis Iles, Carter Dickson, Elizabeth Ferrars, and Gladys Mitchell. Black Dagger Crime can be set up as a standing order plan for your library so that you automatically receive each new title as it is reprinted.

Five Star, an imprint of the Gale Group, is another publisher that has brought back into print mystery titles that were once unavailable. Older titles by Carolyn G. Hart, P. M. Carlson, and Nancy Pickard are now available in attractive library edition hardcovers. Recently, this publisher has been busy gathering short story collections by mystery writers such as Bill Pronzini and Dorothy Salisbury Davis that are then offered as part of Five Star's mystery line.

University presses can also be a valuable resource when it comes to acquiring new editions of long-lost mysteries. In February 2000, the University of Pennsylvania Press offered trade paperback editions of two Daphne du Maurier classic titles, *Scapegoat* and *The House on the Strand,* to tie in with publication of a new biography of du Maurier by a professor at Penn State. The University of Nebraska Press is keeping one of Nebraska's most famous author's works in print by republishing an assortment of titles by mystery Grand Master Mignon G. Eberhart. On a smaller scale, the Afton Historical Society Press has recently brought back into print three titles by Mabel Seeley, "Minnesota's answer to Agatha Christie."

DEADHEADING YOUR MYSTERY COLLECTION

Very few of us enjoy weeding any part of our library's collection. There is always the underlying fear that we will unwittingly discard some classic of the genre and then readers will hate us forever. Well, get over it! It's time to conquer your fears. Weeding is a necessary and critical part of collection development.

Most libraries only have so much room for their mystery collections. Keep adding titles, and eventually you are going to run out of space. Aside from the overcrowding issue, most mystery collections need a regular weeding to keep them looking fresh and attractive to readers.

Like almost anything else, weeding goes more smoothly if you have a plan and some guidelines in place before you start discarding books.

Decide in advance what criteria will be used for weeding a title. Physical condition of the item, circulation history, and number of other copies of the same title are all factors that should be taken into account when weeding mystery books. How frequently you weed your mystery collection will depend a great deal on your own individual institution. Small public libraries, because of space considerations, may need to devote time every year to weeding out their stacks, but a large academic library may choose to weed its mystery collection only every five to ten years.

Weeding mystery titles, as with any other type of fiction, often seems to be a very subjective process. After taking into account such factors as physical condition and circulation history, staff members responsible for weeding mystery fiction may feel like they must pass judgment on titles with little more to go on than the jacket copy and a vague perception as to how popular the book is with readers in their community. Luckily the same genre reference sources that were helpful when you did an assessment of your collection can also be used when you go out to weed the stacks. Classic fiction collection development and readers' advisory titles like *Fiction Catalog* and *Genreflecting* should always be used in weeding fiction collections. In addition to these sources, bring some of your other mystery genre reference titles such as *Detecting Men, Detecting Women,* and *By a Woman's Hand* out in the stacks with you to help identify authors and titles with which you might not be familiar.

You do have a bit more leeway when it comes to weeding mystery fiction than other sections of your collection. Mystery fiction does not have the same timeliness issues as, for example, many nonfiction areas. People still want to read classic mystery authors such as Francis and Richard Lockridge and Margery Allingham, so do not be too quick to pull them out of your collections. Also, whenever possible, try to avoid weeding one title out of a mystery series.

While weeding your mystery collection, give some thought to preservation issues. If you have the ability to send books to be rebound, take advantage of it. Rebinding books is one of the most cost-effective ways of keeping individual titles in your collection. Rebinding is especially valuable for library collections when it comes to out-of-print mystery titles. Books that need minor repairs should also be targeted during your weeding project. If a book can be rejacketed or relabeled, send it to be mended.

Don't forget to keep track of the authors and titles you are weeding so that you can check for new or reprinted editions to replace those you have pulled. Replacing worn and tattered copies of mystery books with new ones can go a long way toward brightening up your library's collection and drawing in new mystery readers.

Librarians new to weeding fiction, as well as those who are old hands at the process but need a refresher, will want to read "Weeding the Fiction Collection; or, Should I Dump *Peyton Place*?" by Merle Jacob (2001). This excellent article covers all of the basics of weeding fiction (not just mysteries) and can serve as a good introduction to the topic.

Unique Factors Affecting Mystery Selection and Collection Development

The first thing librarians encounter when selecting mystery fiction for their collections is the role paperback originals play in this genre. Unfortunately, some librarians have some preconceived prejudices against paperbacks. Whether it is the misguided notion that paperbacks are too fragile and will not hold up to sustained checkouts or the foolish idea that paperbacks are somehow "inferior" to hardcover books, these librarians refuse to purchase paperbacks for their collections. Paperback original mystery fiction, however, is a critical part of this genre, and it is time for hardcover snobs to rise above these dated notions.

Many first-time mystery authors debut in paperback. Jerrilyn Farmer's cozy culinary mysteries and Helen Chappell's humorous series featuring Hollis Ball and Sam Wescott are only available as paperback originals. Are you willing to deprive your patrons of reading these mysteries simply because you have a "thing" about paperback books? In addition, the works of a number of established mystery authors are only available in paperback. Need to add more copies of some of Agatha Christie's or Dorothy Sayers's books? Good luck in finding any of their titles in hardcover. Even the earlier titles by contemporary mystery writers such as Aaron Elkins or Jan Burke are now only available in paperback, so if you need to replace titles in your collection, this is the only edition you can purchase. Depriving mystery readers in your area of these and other authors whose work may only be available in paperback is just criminal.

Another factor that affects the selection and development of your mystery collection is the number of significant mystery titles that are currently out-of-print. Regrettably, other genres, such as romance fiction and fantasy fiction, also suffer from this problem. Selectors looking to add Edgar Award winners from years past will discover that a significant number are currently out-of-print. Even when it comes to classic authors, such as Ellery Queen or Catherine Aird, few titles may be available.

What can the dedicated mystery selector do, other than light a candle or choose to curse the publishing world? The best advice we have is to watch and wait. You never know when a particular author will come back into vogue and be reprinted. In recent years, St. Martin's Press repackaged and reprinted all of Ngaio Marsh's classic mysteries, and Scribner has brought back into print Josephine Tey's marvelous books. Simon and Schuster republished Mary Higgins Clark's first classic suspense novel, *Where Are the Children?* in hardcover as part of its S & S Classic Editions, and in 2001, Scribner added new hardcover editions of P. D. James's two Cordelia Gray mysteries, *An Unsuitable Job for a Woman* and *The Skull beneath the Skin.* You never can tell when and where a particular author or title is going turn up, but publishers' catalogs can be some of the best ways to track these reprint programs.

Another factor affecting mystery fiction selection and collection development is the prevalence of small presses. Drawn to this genre by its popularity with readers, the number of original mystery titles published by small presses increases each year. Small publishers, such as Silver Dagger Mysteries and Perseverance Press (whose recent title *Guns and Roses,* by Taffy Cannon, was a 2000 Edgar Award nominee), are bringing an assortment of new mystery titles to the market. Selectors have several ways to keep up with the output from small presses. Reviews of some small press mysteries can be found in both traditional review sources, such as *Booklist* and *Library Journal,* as well as the more genre-specific periodicals, such as *Mystery News* and *Deadly Pleasures.* Some of the small publishers, such as Silver Dagger Mysteries and Soho Press, have websites with everything you need to know about their new releases in one handy place.

University presses are also getting into the act. The University of New Mexico is Judith Van Gieson's hardcover publisher for her new Claire Reynier mystery series, with the paperback being simultaneously published by Signet. The University Press of Colorado was the first to publish Margaret Coel's *The Eagle Catcher,* which introduced her detective Vicky Holden. *The Hunt for Red October,* Tom Clancy's book that created the techno-thriller craze, was published by Naval Institute Press.

Although it may not come up that often, selectors should be aware that American and British mystery publishing is not always synchronized. Books by mystery authors such as Val McDermid and Lindsey Davis might be published months or even a year earlier in Great Britain than they are in America. (Dedicated fans of Davis's Falco series know this and will frequently splurge and buy the British edition of her books just so they can read it before it is available in the United States.) Another variation on this theme is that some authors who were formerly published in both America and Great Britain are now only being published by the British. Examples of this include authors Kate Charles, Betty Rowlands, and Donna Leon.

Mystery collection development can be a daunting task. Keeping up with current releases, trying to replace missing titles, weeding your collection, and racing through a variety of review sources in search of hidden gems can add up to what seems to be a never-ending job. Fortunately, the time and effort required in building a better mystery collection yield tremendous dividends. The knowledge of your own library's collection can translate into better readers' advisory service for your patrons, who, in turn, are rewarded with the promise that there will always be something mysterious for them to read.

7

Marketing Your Mystery Collection

For decades, many libraries have operated under a *Field of Dreams* theory of collection development: if we buy it, they will come. The foundation of collection development depends first upon the careful selection of library materials. The importance of a well-rounded collection is still the cornerstone of any good library. However, when it comes to attracting new readers to your mystery collection and keeping your present readers interested in and checking out materials, this passive approach is not enough. Effective, proactive marketing of your mystery collection is a must.

The first step in marketing your mystery collection (or any part of your library's collection, for that matter) is getting rid of any general misperceptions you may harbor about marketing. Some librarians feel that marketing carries a whiff of commercialism that should never sully their library's doorstep. Marketing may conjure up images of slick ad campaigns and the scary world of business. At its most basic level, however, marketing is simply a way of drawing attention to a product. In this case, the product is your library's mystery collection and the service of readers' advisory, a service that a large portion of your library patrons may not be aware that you offer. It is important to remember that your library is competing for your patron's time with other recreational opportunities. If you do not at least start to think about ways to market your mystery collection and readers' advisory services, soon you may not have readers for them.

BOOK LISTS AND BIBLIOGRAPHIES; OR, ALWAYS ANNOTATE THE ONES YOU LOVE

One of the most widely used and easiest ways to market a portion of your collection is through a book list or bibliography. (For our purposes here, *book lists* will mean both book lists and bibliographies.) Book lists are your most important marketing tool, and they are often used as a substitute for a library staff member who can offer personal readers' advisory service. Book lists are valuable because they can help alleviate the sense of "overload" some readers may experience by offering these readers a smaller group of titles from which to select. As a marketing tool, book lists must capture and keep a reader's attention long enough to get your message across: "Here are some great books you may want to read."

With very few exceptions, any book lists your library hands out to patrons should be annotated or offer some type of description of the books for the reader. A book list that simply provides a list of authors and titles under a generic heading such as "Good Mysteries" isn't worth the paper it's printed on. Readers want to know something about a book before they are willing to invest their time and effort in locating and reading it.

Handing out this generic type of book list is analogous to a grocery store stocking its shelves with cans that simply say *diet soda* or boxes with only the word *cereal* printed on them and nothing else. With the exception of revealing key plot points or the identity of the murderer, do not be stingy with the amount of information you provide on your mystery book lists.

We all work in the real world, and some librarians may not have time to lovingly annotate each entry in every book list they prepare. However, it is almost always possible to at least provide some information on your book lists for the reader to use. For example, you can group similar types of mysteries together, such as historical mysteries, and then offer some facts about this mystery subgenre. Or provide a few details about the book's detective, its setting, time period, and so forth—anything that readers can use to help them decide whether or not this is a book they might like.

MIX OR MATCH:
COMPILING A SUCCESSFUL BOOK LIST

Most mystery book lists fall into two categories: a mix of various authors and subgenres or a match of one particular type or subgenre. Both of these types of book lists have their value and place: the mixed book list may appeal to a wider audience of readers because there is a little something for every mystery reader to choose from. The matched book list will appeal to a smaller audience of readers, but it will provide them with more reading choices. Plan on having both kinds of book lists available. *See* Figures 2 and 3 for examples of both types of book lists.

Don't be a book list tease! When you are beginning to compile your book list, try to choose titles that your library holds more than one copy of in its collection (or plan on buying additional copies of the title). There is nothing worse for a reader than being presented with several choices of titles and finding out everything he or she wants is checked out and not available for immediate reading consumption.

Once you have selected the books you wish to showcase, you must now write annotations for them. Writing great annotations for book lists is an art, and few of us are gifted with a talent for it, but it does become easier with practice. As an annotator, you are trying to distill the essence of a book into one snappy sentence. Some of the best examples of well-crafted book annotations appear weekly on the *New York Times* bestseller list. With a deliberate economy of words, nearly every annotation offers readers a taste of what the book will be like, and they serve as an excellent model.

As you write your annotation for each book, ask yourself these questions: who is the protagonist? What is the setting? The time period? What obstacles must the hero or heroine overcome? What is the mood of the story? Is it creepy, cozy, humorous, gritty? Always use sharp, memorable words in your annotation, and do not worry too much about achieving grammatical perfection. One of the best guides to crafting annotations, "How to Write a Fiction Annotation," was written by Dorothy M. Broderick (1993). By studying these guidelines and practicing writing annotations, even novice annotators can turn out book lists that will tantalize readers and have them coming back for more!

FIGURE 2

Librarian's Choice

Mystery

May we suggest one of the following titles, which represent the variety of mysteries available to you?

Thyme of Death by Susan Wittig Albert
Abandoning her life as a lawyer in Houston, China Bayles opens an herb shop in Pecan Springs only to find murder can happen even in a small Texas town.

Aunt Dimity's Death by Nancy Atherton
To claim a bequest in a will, American Lori Shepherd travels to England only to discover what she believed to be a fictional character from her childhood stories turns out to have been a real person.

Goodnight, Irene by Jan Burke
When a friend and mentor is killed, newspaper reporter Irene Kelly investigates and finds his death may be related to an old murder case.

A Killing in Quail County by Jameson Cole
In a small Oklahoma town in the 1950s, fifteen-year-old Mark Stoddard and his two friends try to find a bootlegger only to stumble onto a murder.

The Black Echo by Michael Connelly
LAPD Detective Hieronymus "Harry" Bosch investigates the death of a derelict Vietnam veteran who has a connection with Bosch's wartime past.

Postmortem by Patricia Daniels Cornwell
A perplexing case involving a psychopathic murderer draws in medical examiner Kay Scarpetta.

Catering to Nobody by Diane Mott Davidson
When her former father-in-law is nearly poisoned at an affair she catered, Goldy Bear decides to do some sleuthing before the police close down her business permanently.

Principal Defense by Gini Hartzmark
Mergers and acquisitions lawyer Kate Milholland looks for the murderer of a young girl whose corporate shares could determine the fate of a pharmaceutical company fending off a takeover bid.

Murder in Scorpio by Martha C. Lawrence
Private investigator and parapsychologist Elizabeth Chase uses both deduction and intuition when she looks into what seems to be a routine traffic fatality.

A Drink before the War by Dennis Lehane
P.I. partners Patrick Kenzie and Angela Gennaro think it's "easy money" when a Boston politician hires them to track down some stolen documents.

Bootlegger's Daughter by Margaret Maron
While running for district judge, attorney Deborah Knott, the daughter of a retired bootlegger, is asked by Gayle Whitehead to find out who murdered her mom eighteen years ago.

Caught Dead in Philadelphia by Gillian Roberts
Philadelphia schoolteacher Amanda Pepper finds a murdered coworker in her house and the police assuming she had something to do with the crime.

China Trade by S. J. Rozan
A Chinatown museum puts private eye Lydia Chin and her partner, Bill Smith, on retainer when a set of antique porcelain is stolen.

A Cold Day for Murder by Dana Stabenow
Ex-D.A. Kate Shugak has returned to her roots in the Alaska bush but she comes out of retirement to search for a missing park ranger and the guide who went looking for him.

The Red Scream by Mary Willis Walker
After receiving an anonymous letter, Texas crime reporter Molly Cates wonders if a notorious serial killer scheduled for execution is really guilty of all the murders he is accused of committing.

Sunrise by Chassie West
D.C. cop Leigh Anne Warren figures a visit to her small hometown will help her recover from the stress of a difficult case, but then murder intervenes.

For assistance in locating these or other books, please ask at the Information / Reference Desk.

SCOTTSDALE PUBLIC
LIBRARY
SYSTEM

480-312-READ (7323)
http://library.ci.scottsdale.az.us

FIGURE 3

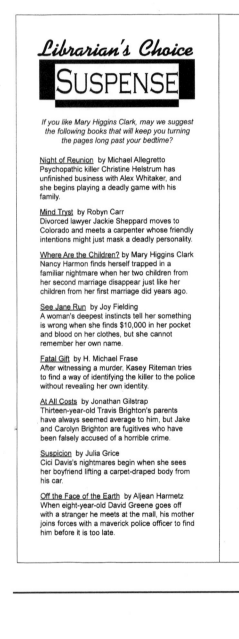

Librarian's Choice

SUSPENSE

If you like Mary Higgins Clark, may we suggest the following books that will keep you turning the pages long past your bedtime?

Night of Reunion by Michael Allegretto
Psychopathic killer Christine Helstrum has unfinished business with Alex Whitaker, and she begins playing a deadly game with his family.

Mind Tryst by Robyn Carr
Divorced lawyer Jackie Sheppard moves to Colorado and meets a carpenter whose friendly intentions might just mask a deadly personality.

Where Are the Children? by Mary Higgins Clark
Nancy Harmon finds herself trapped in a familiar nightmare when her two children from her second marriage disappear just like her children from her first marriage did years ago.

See Jane Run by Joy Fielding
A woman's deepest instincts tell her something is wrong when she finds $10,000 in her pocket and blood on her clothes, but she cannot remember her own name.

Fatal Gift by H. Michael Frase
After witnessing a murder, Kasey Riteman tries to find a way of identifying the killer to the police without revealing her own identity.

At All Costs by Jonathan Gilstrap
Thirteen-year-old Travis Brighton's parents have always seemed average to him, but Jake and Carolyn Brighton are fugitives who have been falsely accused of a horrible crime.

Suspicion by Julia Grice
Cici Davis's nightmares begin when she sees her boyfriend lifting a carpet-draped body from his car.

Off the Face of the Earth by Aljean Harmetz
When eight-year-old David Greene goes off with a stranger he meets at the mall, his mother joins forces with a maverick police officer to find him before it is too late.

Final Tour by Jonellen Heckler
At the height of her career, singer Sass Lindsey decides to retire, but now someone wants to make her retirement permanent.

No Way Home by Patricia MacDonald
Lillie Burdette seeks the truth behind her daughter's death, but the answers she finds threaten both her safety and her sanity.

Fast Forward by Judy Mercer
Ariel Gold wakes up one morning and, after staring into a mirror, realizes she has no idea whose face is looking back at her; she only knows that she is not that woman.

Shattered Silk by Barbara Michaels
While searching for vintage clothing, Karen Nevitt becomes caught up in a web of danger.

Precipice by Tom Savage
A beautiful woman arrives at the Precott's home in tropical St. Thomas and sets into play a deadly game of deception.

Darkness Falls by Joyce Ann Schneider
When a psychiatrist discovers similarities between the murder of a patient and her own mother's death twenty years earlier, she begins her own investigation of the crime.

The Caretaker by Thomas William Simpson
Gunn Henderson accepts a new job that includes the use of a company mansion that comes complete with its very own caretaker.

Someone to Watch Over by Trish Macdonald Skillman
Someone is watching over Kate Eldridge and her two children very carefully, but his concern soon turns into an obsession.

The Way You Look Tonight by Carlene Thompson
Deborah Robinson begins to wonder if her husband's disappearance could be connected to the horrible killings of several local women.

For assistance in locating these or other books, please ask at the Information / Reference Desk.

SCOTTSDALE PUBLIC
LIBRARY
SYSTEM

480-312-READ (7323)
http://library.ci.scottsdale.az.us

Although there is no "magic" number of entries for a book list, a good number to work with is generally ten to thirty titles. Any fewer than ten and readers go through the book list too quickly. Any more than thirty entries and readers may feel overwhelmed by the number of titles from which to choose.

While you are compiling your book list, remember that the layout of the book list will be affected by how and where it is displayed. Traditional bookmark-sized book lists can easily be tucked inside books. Full-sized booklet-type book lists may work better in display units. If you are fortunate enough to have a graphics person working in your library, be sure you consult with him or her from the moment you begin planning a new book list. Don't forget that space must be left on a book list if you are going to add any graphic elements.

Once you have completed your mystery book list, your work with that particular handout is still not done. Every book list your library offers to its patrons should be updated and revised on a regular basis. Most book lists have a shelf life ranging from two to five years and will need to be revised or rewritten to keep them fresh and useful for the reader. When revising, it is a good idea to evaluate how successful the book list has been with your readers. A book list focusing on a particular mystery subgenre may not be as popular as it once was, and there might not be the need to update that particular handout.

Although most of us immediately think of book lists in a traditional way as a printed handout, a number of libraries are taking book lists into the future by posting them onto their libraries' Web catalogs. This type of book list offers readers a unique advantage in that by pointing and clicking on a particular title, readers can immediately discover if that book is available. Readers can choose titles on a book list directly from home, even before they have set foot in the library. *See* Figure 4 for seven basics to remember when creating a book list or bibliography.

DISPLAYS—WHAT ARE YOU LOOKING AT?

The layout of your library will play the largest role in determining the type of displays you can mount. Some libraries may have built-in display cases or special areas devoted to merchandising their collection. Other

---

FIGURE 4
Book List and Bibliography Basics

1. Think about where and how your book list or bibliography will be displayed or handed out. This can affect the format.

2. Choose a theme or topic: a similar type of books or a mixed group.

3. Select titles that you have enough copies of in your system to satisfy demand.

4. Between ten to thirty different titles is a good number to work with.

5. Almost all book lists and bibliographies should be annotated. Keep your annotations to a sentence or two in length per book. For good examples of annotations, check the *New York Times* best-seller list.

6. Remember, whenever possible, book lists and bibliographies can be a part of your library's Web page.

7. Book lists and bibliographies should be updated and revised on a regular basis.

---

libraries may have the space to set up tables or exhibits and not impact the flow of traffic. Before you begin assembling a display in your library, take a look around and see what you have to work with.

Libraries generally put together two different types of displays. One kind is meant to showcase a portion of the collection and bring various authors and titles to the attention of readers. Think of this as the store-window type of display or the look-but-do-not-touch approach. The other category of display is meant to encourage patrons to pick books up from the display itself. This is the open type of interactive display you might see inside a bookstore.

Once you have taken stock of your library's display possibilities and decided which type of display you wish to mount, now comes the creative part. Determine the scope or theme of the display. Are you going to showcase a particular subgenre of mysteries, such as private detective novels, or are you going to put together a display featuring mysteries of a similar type, such as pet mysteries? As you develop and refine the scope of your mystery display, be sure that your library has enough materials on your theme to keep the display going. This is particularly important in an open display. If you only have a small number of titles on a particular theme and they check out quickly, your display can soon look threadbare and uninviting. Once you have begun doing displays on a regular basis, you will discover that readers grow to trust the quality of books you put on display, so make a point of choosing titles for your display carefully. Your readers deserve the best you can offer them!

One display our library did focused on the centennial celebration of Dorothy Sayers. We gathered together copies of all of Sayers's mysteries, biographies of the author, and books of literary criticism that featured her mysteries. After we placed these books in our display case, we added other objects, such as a teapot and teacups, lace doilies, a pair of women's gloves, and a chapeau from the era, to give the display texture. A map of England was placed at the back of the display to serve as a backdrop, and several short quotes from Sayers's books and writings were matted and hung in the case. The final touch was a sign placed in the center of the display encouraging readers to "Celebrate the Sayers Centennial."

If your creative well has gone dry, consider some of these possibilities:

Culinary Crimes

Pull together mysteries featuring a cooking theme, such as those by Diane Mott Davidson, Virginia Rich, and Katherine Hall Page (for more authors, *see* the "Culinary Crimes" book list in appendix B, page 165). Think about adding some favorite cookbooks to the display as well. Don't forget to add some clever props, such as a chef's hat, cooking utensils, and an apron!

Crime around the Country or World

Using a large U.S. or world map as a backdrop, pick mysteries that prominently feature a specific country or city. Put markers in the map indicating which mysteries are set there. For more inspiration and ideas of authors and titles to use, check out *Crimes of the Scene: A Mystery Novel Guide for the International Traveler,* by Nina King, with Robin Winks, or Marvin Lachman's *The American Regional Mystery.* Many other mystery reference books, such as *Detecting Women* and *Detecting Men*, both by Willetta L. Heising, have geographic indexes. The April 15, 1997, issue of *Booklist* has an excellent "Hard-Boiled Gazetteer to the U.S." with dozens of mystery authors and titles.

Classic Crimes

This can be a wonderful chance to introduce your patrons to the classic mystery writers of the late nineteenth and twentieth centuries. Although the books of Agatha Christie and Raymond Chandler may be old news to some mystery readers, many others have never experienced the joy of reading Christie's clever plotting or meeting Rex Stout's eccentric sleuth, Nero Wolfe. Put some biographies of the authors in with their books and some literary criticism books, too. Some authors to consider include Ngaio Marsh, Dorothy Sayers, Sir Arthur Conan Doyle, John Dickson Carr, Ellery Queen, and Edgar Allan Poe (for more authors to include, *see* the "Classic Mysteries" book list in appendix B, page 154).

Historical Crimes

Mix and match historical mysteries with real history books and biographies of famous people. For example, display copies of Stephanie Barron's Jane Austen mysteries with various biographies of Austen and works of literary criticism. Biographies of Eleanor Roosevelt are a natural pairing with Elliot Roosevelt's mysteries featuring the famous first lady. Elizabethan mysteries by authors such as Karen Harper, Fiona Buckley, and Edward Marston would work wonderfully with nonfiction titles on that era and its queen (for more choices, *see* the "Historical Mysteries" book list in appendix A, page 120).

Noir

Try this great way to promote classic film noir stories such as Raymond Chandler's *The Big Sleep* or James Cain's *The Postman Always Rings Twice,* in addition to modern-day authors such as Max Allan Collins, whose Nathan Heller series uses a historical setting. Use old movie posters as an attention-grabbing backdrop, and mix and match books about old Hollywood from the 1930s and 1940s to stimulate interest in both areas. If your library makes videos or DVDs available for checkout, be sure to include some classic noir titles, too. (For more noir choices to add to your display, *see* our "Fiction Noir and Neo-Noir" book list in appendix B, page 171.)

Finishing Touches

When you are planning a mystery display, don't forget to include some texture in the display. Simply propping up books on a table will not draw many readers. Consider adding some props (especially if you can affix them securely), and check with your coworkers to see if they might have anything they can lend. Don't forget to have copies of your mystery book lists nearby or, if appropriate, in the display itself to help cross-pollinate interest in your mystery collection. Be sure that your display has some type of signage to clue your patrons in as to what you are doing.

As noted above, if you are considering doing a closed display (i.e., a display in which patrons may not take books from the display itself), ensure you have at least two or more copies of the display books available for checkout. There is nothing worse for a reader than to discover a great book in your display and then to be told that he or she cannot check the book out until after the display comes down.

If you decide to put together an open display of mystery books, you must factor in the amount of time it will take each day to maintain the display. You or your coworkers will need to restock books on display and tidy up things periodically to keep the display fresh and attractive to browsers

The ability to create attractive, vibrant displays is a gift, but it is possible to improve what display skills you have through practice and by taking advantage of any of your coworkers who may have ideas and suggestions for great displays. One way to become more aware of display possibilities is to visit your local bookstores and see how they set up and maintain their displays. Ask them for any hints or tips they may have that can help you.

PROGRAMMING

For libraries that have the staff and time, adult programming can be another effective means of marketing your library's mystery collection.

The range of programming possibilities is only limited by your library's budget and staff considerations. Programs can be done with a low-key approach with limited time or money or both or in an elaborate, time-intensive manner. Both methods can lead to successful programs.

Mystery Book Discussion Groups: Talk amongst Yourselves

The last decade has seen a renaissance of book discussion programs in libraries, bookstores, and private homes. A book discussion group focusing specifically on mystery fiction can be one of your library's most popular types of programs. As with any book discussion program, you need to do your homework first. Try to determine what will be the best day and time to hold your discussion group meetings. For some libraries, a weekday night may work best; other libraries find a weekend morning or afternoon discussion group draws more people. Before you even start thinking about what books to discuss, be sure you understand the basics of how book discussion groups work. There are a number of excellent general guides to starting a book discussion group, including *The Book Group Book: A Thoughtful Guide to Forming and Enjoying a Stimulating Book Discussion Group,* by Ellen Slezak; *The Reading Group Book: The Complete Guide to Starting and Sustaining a Reading Group, with Annotated Lists of 250 Titles for Provocative Discussion,* by David Laskin and Holly Hughes; and *The Reading Group Handbook: Everything You Need to Know, from Choosing Members to Leading Discussions,* by Rachel W. Jacobsohn. Readers' advisory librarians will particularly want to check out *The Complete Idiot's Guide to Starting a Reading Group,* by Patrick Sauer, because it includes an entertaining chapter on mystery fiction and book discussion groups.

Once you have absorbed the basics of hosting a discussion group, you are ready to start choosing some mystery titles. Because the keyword in book discussion groups is *discussion,* it is important to pick titles that will provoke lively interaction from those attending. Unfortunately, some mystery books, though highly enjoyable and delightful to read, just do not lend themselves well to the book discussion venue. Mysteries such as those by John Grisham or Lilian Braun are designed to entertain readers and may not serve as the foundation for serious discussions. Some mystery authors will work better for this purpose. Mysteries to consider for a book discussion group might include Martha Lawrence's *Hearts and Bones,* an intense historical mystery that offers the opportunity to discuss such topics as women's roles in postrevolutionary America and the effect the American Revolution had on people in the fledging country (readers will be fascinated to learn that post-traumatic stress disorder did not originate with the Vietnamese conflict).

In some cases, a particular title by one author might be a better choice than another book by the same person. For example, P. D. James is known for her mystery series featuring Adam Dalgliesh, as well as her two Cordelia Gray mysteries. But it is her standalone title *Innocent Blood,* the story of an adopted young woman who discovers exactly who her real parents were, that may offer so much more for a group to discuss.

Some discussion groups may want to select a mystery by an author such as Raymond Chandler, who is known as much for his literate writing style as he is for his plots and characters. Or Dorothy Sayers's mysteries can provide much material for a good discussion leader to work with. (For more mysteries suitable for a book discussion group, *see* our book list in appendix B, page 157.)

An interesting twist on the traditional book discussion group is to pair up a mystery title with its companion mystery video. A number of excellent films have been based on mystery books. Just a few examples include *The Postman Always Rings Twice, The Talented Mr. Ripley, L.A. Confidential,* and *Rebecca.* Beginning your discussion with a talk about the inevitable changes between the novel and the film is one of the easiest ways to break the ice. Use a reference source such as Otto Penzler's *101 Greatest Films of Mystery and Suspense* to identify possible titles, keeping in mind their availability in video format, and you can come up with a series of exciting matchups.

Although this tip seems quite obvious, it's an important one: be aware of the availability of a particular mystery title before selecting it for a large group. If the title you wish to discuss is out-of-print and you only have a few copies of the book in your library's collection, it might be frustrating for those who wish to read the book before the discussion.

Some book discussion groups may enjoy "hosting" an author for one of their meetings. Areas with a large number of local mystery authors or those cities that draw authors on book tours may especially be attracted to this concept. Reading a book by an author and then having the opportunity to get an inside look at how the book developed can be entertaining and enlightening. However, having an author present while your group discusses his or her mystery can also present come unique challenges. Some group members might be reluctant to openly talk about things they felt did not work for them as readers of the book if the author is on hand. Some authors may find it difficult to listen as readers critique their "baby." Each discussion group will need to sort these pros and cons out carefully before inviting an author to sit in on a discussion.

Author Programs; or, Up Close and Personal

Hosting a mystery author program at your library can either be one of the most enjoyable and successful programs you have or it can be a nightmare. It is up to you as to which way it turns out. Readers love to hear authors speak about their work, and many authors enjoy interacting with readers, but if you want to increase the odds that your author program is a success, heed the following steps.

The most important ingredient in your author program is the author himself or herself. Choosing the right author for your program requires advance planning, a certain amount of flexibility, and a little bit of luck. Libraries looking for mystery authors as possible speakers should consider the following resource: Sisters in Crime, a national association of mystery writers, readers, librarians, and booksellers, annually publishes a listing of its members' books in print that includes a geographic index.

First and foremost, not all authors are comfortable speaking in front of groups. If an author seems reluctant or shy to do a program for your library, respect his or her wishes and don't try to coax the author into doing so. There is nothing worse than watching someone muddle his or her way through a talk when both you and your audience know that the speaker would rather be anywhere else than standing in front of them, pretending to enjoy talking to groups.

On the other hand, if your library is approached by an author to do a program, you need to do a little checking first. Ask the author if he or she has done programs for any other groups or bookstores in the area. If possible, contact these groups and see how the program went. Your responsibility to your patrons is to provide a well-planned, entertaining program. It may be necessary at times to gently and politely dissuade an author from doing a program if you do not feel it will be the least bit successful.

Your library's programming facilities will also play a part in the author you should consider. If you only have a small space that will seat fewer than 25 people, you do not want to try and book an author like Sue Grafton, who will attract a large crowd. Conversely, if your auditorium seats 300 people, asking a new, relatively unknown mystery author to speak is a disadvantage. Although the program may attract a respectable number of people, seeing them scattered in such a large setting may disappoint or intimidate the author. Match whatever programming spaces you have with the anticipated audience and speaker you hope to attract.

Once you have confirmed an author as a speaker, both parties involved need to understand the expectations for the program and agree on how things will be done. First determine what type of program you will be offering. Is it simply going to be a book signing with the author chatting with readers as they sign books? Or is the author going to provide a formal talk? What is the time frame of the program? Who will be responsible for publicity for the program? Who is the target audience? Does the author have a speaking fee that needs to be budgeted for? Will the author expect the library to cover travel expenses?

If you are planning on combining an author talk with a book signing by the author, determine in advance who will be providing the books for the signing. If the author is bringing copies, will he or she need help selling books? Will you need to plan on having change available for those people who do not have exact change? If the library is responsible for providing the books, determine how you will obtain copies.

Refreshments may be another consideration for some library mystery programs. If food and drink will be served at your author program, plan early on who will provide the refreshments, who will help set up for the program, and who will help with cleanup after the program. If you can convince a coworker or a volunteer to help out with this part of the program, it will leave you free to concentrate on the author.

Once you have the details down for your author program, you will need to start thinking of ways to publicize the program. In addition to any publicity materials your individual library may hand out, consider sending information on the program to local bookstores, any local chapters of national mystery groups, such as Sisters in Crime, and local colleges or universities. Once you have done a program or two, you will begin to develop an idea of what works for your library publicitywise and what does not.

It is a good idea at least a week or two before the program to confirm the speaking arrangement with your guest author. Ask if he or she needs directions and be prepared to offer instructions on parking. Verify any last-minute details with the author such as whether he or she will need an introduction, if he or she will be bringing guests, and so forth.

On the day of the program itself, plan on arriving early. Check to see that the seating arrangements are what you have in mind. If refreshments are being served, see to it that these preparations are under way. If your author will be signing books, have a separate table set up for the signing with several pens ready. If you are responsible for providing the books, set a few copies out with the other copies nearby. Whenever possible, have another staff member or volunteer standing by to greet those attending the program and to keep an eye out for your author.

Once your author has arrived, greet him or her and take a moment to go over any last-minute arrangements. Gently remind the author of the time frame of the program, and tell him or her that you will give a signal once it is time to wrap up the program. Keeping track of the time your program will run is important. Once in a while an author may become so excited and involved in the talk that he or she forgets how much time has gone by. For some programs, it may be up to you to keep things on track.

For programs where the author will be speaking and taking questions, some libraries might want to keep this trick in mind. Have someone (this can be a staff member, a friend, etc.) planted in the audience with a few prepared questions. Sometimes it takes another person to break the ice before others will ask questions and interact with the author.

Every librarian's worst nightmare is to carefully plan a program, publicize it, attract a good audience, and then not have your speaker show up. In this case, you have few options. If the speaker cannot be reached and you have waited enough time that your audience is getting restless, the best thing to do is to be honest with them. Apologize for the speaker's absence, and thank the audience for taking time to attend.

Some librarians may feel comfortable offering their audience a substitute for the planned speaker. It could be another library staff member who is available to do a spur-of-the-moment mystery booktalk.

Be sure to thank your author after the program, and always send a written follow-up thank-you note. Successful author programs can be a lot of work, but with practice you will find yourself enjoying these types of programs. *See* Figure 5 for a list of tips on hosting authors.

FIGURE 5
Hosting an Author Event

1. Whenever possible, contact the author at least six months to one year in advance of your program.

2. Be sure there is a clear understanding between your library and the author about any possible fees involved in the program.

3. Determine if the author or publisher prefers to make travel arrangements or if your library must do so.

4. Be absolutely sure that you and the author have agreed on the content of the program, its length, and the type of audience the program is directed toward.

5. Check to see if there is any special equipment the author will need for the program (e.g., microphone, overhead projector, etc.) and if the room is to be set up in a special way (e.g., theater seating, classroom seating, etc.).

6. Confirm that the author is willing to sign copies of his or her books. If so, determine who is responsible for providing and selling copies of the books.

7. After all program details have been set, send a letter to the author recapping your agreement.

8. Ask the author or the publisher to send a copy of the author's biography and a list of his or her works to help you with publicity.

9. Get the word out about your program. Use whatever resources you have available, be it your library calendar of events, your library's Web page, the local newspaper, and so forth.

10. Have coworkers or volunteers lined up in advance to help with the program.

11. After the program is over, remember to send a thank-you to your author and the publisher.

Booktalking—Sell That Book!

It is not uncommon to find that there is some confusion in the minds of both patrons and librarians when it comes to a booktalk. It is important to note that a booktalk and a book review are not the same thing. At its most basic, a booktalk is a commercial for books. It's a way of tempting readers into picking up a title they might ordinarily pass by. A booktalk doesn't delve into the critical merits of an individual book or explore its author's place in the literature. This is what a book review does. As Patrick Jones says in *Connecting Young Adults and Libraries,* a booktalk is not "a book review, literary criticism, or a public reading" (1998, 246). Your job as a booktalker is to intrigue your listener into wanting to read these mysteries. You will find audiences immensely enjoy the booktalk experience, far more, perhaps, than they would a scholarly book review.

As a fiction genre, mysteries lend themselves very well to booktalking. They have exciting plots, interesting characters, and great "hooks" (also known in the mystery world as the "macguffin," or thing—whether it's information, an object, money, and so forth—that propels the plot forward). A booktalk program with a mystery theme can include a gamut of titles in subgenres from historical to private eye, and by including a variety of mysteries in your booktalk, you are more likely to offer choices that will appeal to all of your listeners. Presenting a booktalk, whether as an outreach or an internal program, is a great way to excite readers about your library's mystery collection.

There are some excellent how-to titles on the basics of booktalking, including *Tales of Love and Terror: Booktalking the Classics, Old and New,* by Hazel Rochman, and *Connecting Young Adults and Libraries,* by Patrick Jones, which should be the starting point for any librarian planning a booktalk. Although many of these titles are aimed at booktalking to a specific audience, such as young adults, this in no way lessens their usefulness. Indeed, a number of adult mysteries can be successfully booktalked to teens, and what works for that audience will certainly also work for an adult audience.

THE SEVEN COMMANDMENTS OF AN EXCELLENT BOOKTALK

1. *Don't booktalk any mystery you have not read or don't like.*

   You can't be sincere or genuine about a book if you are winging it from the Amazon.com synopsis. Thus, it automatically follows that you don't booktalk a mystery you hate. There are plenty of mysteries out there you like, if not love, and again, you can't genuinely sell a book to other readers if you yourself didn't enjoy it.

2. *Don't give too much away.*

A booktalk isn't a lengthy description of the book's plot; it's an introduction to the story. This is especially true with mysteries. You will not endear yourself to your audience if you spoil the surprise of the story for them.

3. *Refrain from reading from the mystery itself.*

Very few of us are talented enough to give the kind of readings that keep an audience on the edge of its seat. Reading from the book itself usually takes too much time and actually defeats the purpose of tantalizing your audience.

4. *Don't spend too much time on one book.*

Try to keep the amount of time you spend on each individual title to about three to five minutes. Remember to include a variety of mystery titles in your booktalk program. Not every title will be to every listener's taste, but by covering at least five to ten titles from a range of mystery subgenres, you will have included something for almost everyone. Don't make the mistake of booktalking a title for which you only have one copy in your library. You have just created a frustrating situation when more than one listener, fired up by your booktalk, wants to read that specific title right now.

5. *Think visually.*

If at all possible, bring the actual books. Hold each one up as you talk about it (this also gives those of us who are nervous about speaking something to do with our hands) so that your listeners can see the cover art. As you finish talking about each book, hand it to a member of your audience so that it can be passed from listener to listener or place the book upright on a table near you where it can be seen.

6. *Compile a bibliography of the titles you are booktalking.*

Be sure to include title and author information for each book so that your listeners can take the bibliography with them to the library and use it to find those books. If possible, adding even a one-line annotation helps your audience remember which book is which. Take advantage of the booktalk to also offer any other bibliographies and book lists you might have on hand. It's a thoughtful service and great advertising for your library.

7. *Above all, enjoy the experience!*

It is great fun to share your love of mysteries by talking about them. You will find that your booktalk programs are very much appreciated.

Other Types of Programs

Occasionally, a library may find itself in the position of planning and hosting a mystery conference. This will be a rare occurrence for all but the largest public or academic library because the staff time needed for this type of program is considerable, but it is something to keep in mind. Often in this case, a library may partner with a local mystery bookstore to cosponsor the conference. One example of this type of mystery programming is the Mayhem in the Midlands mystery conference, which is cosponsored by the Omaha Public Library and Lincoln City Libraries.

A different type of program opportunity arises with state library association conferences. If you have the chance to suggest or plan a program for your state library conference, consider offering a program featuring a mystery author or authors. Many local mystery authors are delighted to speak to librarians. Not only will you be introducing them to new readers, you will also help promote goodwill between the authors and the library community.

All too often, when libraries plan programs featuring the mystery genre, they focus exclusively on books. Don't forget about the other formats that the mystery genre can take. The medium of film is particularly rich in opportunities for programs. A program devoted to the work of Alfred Hitchcock could feature a speaker from a local college film department as well as offer the opportunity to show some of the master's classic films (always check on public performing rights). Film festivals could be planned around the works of Sir Arthur Conan Doyle or Agatha Christie. These are just a few of the possibilities open to libraries wishing to expand their programming choices by utilizing the range and depth of the mystery genre.

A

Mystery Book Lists by Subgenre

If there is one thing that can start an argument among readers, it's a list of recommended books. Remember the brouhaha when Random House released the "100 Best Novels of the Century" list, and how everyone connected with books, including librarians, teachers, readers, reviewers, publishers, and booksellers, all weighed in with an opinion? It just goes to show that people have strong feelings about book lists, and we are no exception.

How did we come to choose these titles for our lists? We didn't set out to create definitive lists, and we know that many favorite books have not been included. What we did was compile some contemporary titles, some classic titles, some award winners, and still keep the lists short—twenty-five titles or less. We planned the lists for comfortable use by both experienced and novice readers' advisors. A descriptive line or two follows each title, because we absolutely believe that every book list should be annotated.

We encourage the use of these book lists in any format. Use them as a springboard to create your own lists. Your readers will love your book lists and ask for more.

AMATEUR SLEUTHS

Albert, Susan Wittig. *Thyme of Death.* 1992

Abandoning her life as a lawyer in Houston, China Bayles opens an herb shop in Pecan Springs only to find murder can happen even in a small Texas town.

Beck, K. K. *A Hopeless Case.* 1992

Jane da Silva leaves her career as a lounge singer in Europe and returns to Seattle to run her uncle's foundation, which specializes in righting wrongs.

Berry, Carole. *The Letter of the Law.* 1987

When one of the senior partners at the law firm she works at is murdered, office temp Bonnie Indermill wonders if it isn't time to start looking for a new job.

Block, Lawrence. *Burglars Can't Be Choosers.* 1977

Burglar Bernie Rhodenbarr is hired to break into an apartment and steal a box but instead finds a dead body.

Burke, Jan. *Goodnight, Irene.* 1993

When a friend and mentor is killed, newspaper reporter Irene Kelly investigates and finds his death may be related to an old murder case.

Caudwell, Sarah. *Thus Was Adonis Murdered.* 1981

A group of British barristers tries to help a friend when she is accused of murdering a man she spent the night with while on vacation in Venice.

Chappell, Helen. *Slow Dancing with the Angel of Death.* 1996

Reporter Hollis Ball's former husband turns up as a ghost to tell her his apparently accidental death was really murder.

Cooper, Susan Rogers. *One, Two, What Did Daddy Do?* 1992

When the father of a neighboring family is accused of murdering everyone in his family except his youngest child, E. J. Pugh begins her own investigation into the crime.

Cross, Amanda. *In the Last Analysis.* 1964

English professor Kate Fansler needs lawyer Reed Amhearst's help when a student is found murdered.

Dobson, Joanne. *Quieter than Sleep.* 1997

Emily Dickinson scholar Karen Pelletier offers the police a hand investigating the murders of another professor and student.

Dunning, John. *Booked to Die.* 1992

After quitting the police force and opening a bookstore, Cliff Janeway finds himself playing detective again when a book scout is found murdered.

Elkins, Aaron. *Fellowship of Fear.* 1982

While lecturing in Europe, American anthropology professor Gideon Oliver finds his academic skills useful when it comes to finding out who is threatening him.

Fowler, Earlene. *Fool's Puzzle.* 1994

Benni Harper, a recently widowed rancher's wife and San Celina's Folk Art Museum curator, pursues her own inquiry when an artist is found dead in the museum.

Francis, Dick. *Dead Cert.* 1962

Jockey Alan York discovers that champion steeplechase rider Bill Anderson's death during a race was no accident.

Gash, Jonathan. *The Judas Pair.* 1977

British antiques dealer Lovejoy hunts for a legendary pair of dueling pistols that may have been the motive for two murders.

Handler, David. *The Man Who Died Laughing.* 1988

Writer Stewart "Hoagy" Hoag accepts a job ghostwriting the memoirs of one-half of a famous comedy team only to be forced into the role of amateur detective when his client is murdered.

Hartzmark, Gini. *Principal Defense.* 1992

Mergers and acquisitions lawyer Kate Millholland looks for the murderer of a young girl whose corporate shares could determine the fate of a pharmaceutical company trying to fend off a takeover attempt.

Hess, Joan. *Strangled Prose.* 1986

Claire Malloy hosts a book-signing party for romance author Azalea Twilight but soon finds out the author's latest novel contains secrets someone does not want revealed.

McCrumb, Sharyn. *Sick of Shadows.* 1984

Elizabeth MacPherson uncovers plenty of suspects in her cousin's wedding party after the bride-to-be is found murdered.

Pickard, Nancy. *Generous Death.* 1984

Foundation director Jenny Cain wants to know who is murdering local benefactors.

Roberts, Gillian. *Caught Dead in Philadelphia.* 1987

Philadelphia schoolteacher Amanda Pepper comes home to find a murdered coworker in her house and the police assuming she had something to do with the crime.

Rothenberg, Rebecca. *The Bulrush Murders.* 1991

Microbiologist Claire Sharples leaves the East Coast for a job in the San Joaquin Valley and winds up not only trying to find a solution for peach rot, but solving a murder as well.

Walker, Mary Willis. *The Red Scream.* 1994

After receiving an anonymous letter, Texas crime reporter Molly Cates wonders if a notorious serial killer scheduled for execution really is guilty of all the murders he is accused of committing.

PRIVATE INVESTIGATOR MYSTERIES

Barnes, Linda. *A Trouble of Fools.* 1987

Boston private eye Carlotta Carlyle's "simple" missing person case turns out to be connected to the IRA.

Brown, Fredric. *The Fabulous Clipjoint.* 1947

Ambrose Brown, former carnival pitchman currently working as a private investigator, helps his nephew Ed solve the murder of his brother, Wally Brown.

Chandler, Raymond. *The Big Sleep.* 1939

Philip Marlowe becomes enmeshed in a tangled web of deceit and murder when he investigates a blackmail case for degenerate General Sternwood.

Crais, Robert. *The Monkey's Raincoat.* 1987

L.A. private eyes Elvis Cole and Joe Pike find that a seemingly easy case of a missing person is anything but straightforward.

Crumley, James. *The Mexican Tree Duck.* 1993

Loose-cannon Montana private investigator C. W. Shugrue is hired to locate a biker's straight-arrow mother.

Dawson, Janet. *Kindred Crimes.* 1990

Jeri Howard finds the case of a vanished wife, who emptied the joint bank account and dumped her baby with her mother-in-law, is connected to a past tragedy.

Doolittle, Jerome. *Body Scissors.* 1990

Ex-wrestler Tom Bethany is hired to investigate the background of a potential secretary of state.

Grafton, Sue. *"A" Is for Alibi.* 1982

Nikki Fife claims to have been unjustly convicted of murder and retains Kinsey Millhone to discover the real killer and clear her name.

Hammett, Dashiell. *The Maltese Falcon.* 1930

San Francisco P.I. Sam Spade's partner has just been killed—can there be a connection with the beautiful redhead who begs for Spade's help?

Hansen, Joseph. *Fadeout.* 1970

California private investigator Dave Brandstetter isn't convinced a famous folksinger died in a car wreck—for one thing, the body is missing.

Haywood, Gar Anthony. *Fear of the Dark.* 1988

Electrician-turned-private-eye Aaron Gunner is hired not only to find the white man who killed two black men, but to establish the motive behind the murders.

Healy, Jeremiah. *Blunt Darts.* 1984

Private investigator John Francis Cuddy is hired to find the son of a prominent Boston judge by the boy's grandmother.

James, P. D. *An Unsuitable Job for a Woman.* 1972

When her partner commits suicide and leaves her sole proprietor of Pryde's Detective Agency, Cordelia Gray must prove herself as a private investigator.

Katz, Jon. *Death by Station Wagon.* 1993

Househusband and part-time suburban P.I. Kit Deleeuw is hired by local teens to find the truth about the death of a high school couple.

Lacy, Ed. *Room to Swing.* 1957

Toussaint Marcus Moore is hired to keep tabs on a suspected rapist but then must track down a killer when he finds the rapist dead and he is accused of the man's murder.

Lawrence, Martha C. *Murder in Scorpio.* 1995

Private investigator and parapsychologist Elizabeth Chase uses both deduction and intuition when she looks into what seems to be a routine traffic fatality.

Lehane, Dennis. *A Drink before the War.* 1994

P.I. partners Patrick Kenzie and Angela Gennaro think it's easy money when a Boston politician hires them to track down some stolen documents.

Lippman, Laura. *Baltimore Blues*. 1997

Ex-newspaperwoman Tess Monaghan knows her friend "Rock" Paxton is innocent of murdering a prominent Baltimore attorney— but how to prove it?

MacDonald, Ross. *The Moving Target*. 1949

Lew Archer accepts the case of tracking down a missing eccentric California millionaire.

Muller, Marcia. *Edwin of the Iron Shoes*. 1977

The death of an antique dealer finds San Francisco investigator Sharon McCone following a trail that appears to lead to a prestigious museum.

Paretsky, Sara. *Indemnity Only*. 1982

Blue-collar private eye V.I. Warshawski is hired to locate a missing person but instead finds murder, manipulation, and insurance fraud.

Parker, Robert. *The Godwulf Manuscript*. 1973

When tough private investigator Spenser is hired to retrieve a stolen manuscript, he finds the paper trail leads to murder.

Rozan, S. J. *China Trade*. 1994

A Chinatown museum hires private eye Lydia Chin and her partner, Bill Smith, when a set of antique porcelain is stolen.

Valin, Jonathan. *The Lime Pit*. 1980

What seems like a straightforward case develops complications when an elderly man hires Harry Stoner to locate his runaway teenage girlfriend.

Wesley, Valerie Wilson. *When Death Comes Stealing*. 1994

Single mother Tamara Hayle retired from the police force thinking that private investigation would be less dangerous—but she changes her mind when her ex-husband hires her to find a link that connects the deaths of his two sons.

POLICE PROCEDURAL MYSTERIES

Bland, Eleanor Taylor. *Dead Time.* 1992

A death at a flophouse has Detective Marti MacAllister and her partner looking for the only witnesses to murder—two runaway children.

Connelly, Michael. *The Black Echo.* 1992

L.A.P.D. Detective Hieronymus "Harry" Bosch investigates the death of a derelict Vietnam veteran who has a connection to Bosch's wartime past.

Cooper, Susan Rogers. *The Man in the Green Chevy.* 1988

A serial rapist who targets elderly women is only one of the cases Chief Deputy Milt Kovak is working on.

Cornwell, Patricia. *Postmortem.* 1990

A perplexing case involving a psychopathic murderer draws in medical examiner Kay Scarpetta.

Crombie, Deborah. *A Share in Death.* 1993

Detective Inspector Duncan Kincaid goes on vacation to recover from his stressful job only to find murder and mayhem don't go on holiday.

Dunlap, Susan. *Karma.* 1981

Berkeley cop Jill Smith knows it's more than just bad karma when a guru is murdered.

Gilbert, Michael. *The Killing of Katie Steelstock.* 1980

Young Detective Sergeant McCourt is on the case when a popular television star is murdered, but so is the ambitious Chief Superintendent Charlie Knott.

Graham, Caroline. *The Killings at Badger's Drift.* 1988

The unexpected death of an elderly woman in the tiny English town of Badger's Drift has Chief Inspector Barnaby looking for clues.

Harvey, John. *Lonely Hearts.* 1989

Detective Inspector Charlie Resnick is on the trail of a killer who uses "lonely hearts" ads to locate his victims.

Hightower, Lynn S. *Flashpoint.* 1995

Before a man dies from a car fire, he tells police specialist Sonora Blake that the fire was not an accident and that a woman set it.

Hill, Reginald. *A Clubbable Woman.* 1970

When a rugby player's wife is killed, Superintendent Dalziel and Detective Sergeant Pascoe are on the case.

Hillerman, Tony. *Dancehall of the Dead.* 1973

A Zuni Indian boy is dead, and a missing Navajo Indian boy is falsely accused as the culprit, according to Navajo policeman Joe Leaphorn.

Jance, J. A. *Until Proven Guilty.* 1985

Seattle Detective J. P. Beaumont is suspicious of the cult to which a dead five-year-old and her mother belong.

King, Laurie R. *Grave Talent.* 1993

Detective Kate Martinelli becomes emotionally involved while working on a heartbreaking case of child homicide in the hills outside San Francisco.

Mathews, Francine. *Death in the Off-Season.* 1994

When a man's body is found in a cranberry bog on picturesque Nantucket Island, third-generation cop Merry Folger is assigned the murder investigation.

Mayor, Archer. *Open Season.* 1998

When the jurors who sat on a high-profile case begin dying, Lieutenant Joe Gunther discovers that even a small town in Vermont can't escape big-city violence.

McBain, Ed. *Cop Hater.* 1956

Detective Steve Carella of the 87th Precinct is on a grim search for a cop killer.

O'Connell, Carol. *Mallory's Oracle.* 1994

Detective Kathleen Mallory's beat isn't on the streets; it's the world of modems and megabytes.

O'Donnell, Lillian. *The Phone Calls.* 1972

An anonymous caller who terrorizes women challenges N.Y.P.D. rookie Norah Mulcahaney.

Rankin, Ian. *Knots and Crosses.* 1987

Edinburgh detective John Rebus solves a complex murder case only to find he has made an implacable enemy.

Robinson, Peter. *The Gallows View.* 1987

Chief Inspector Alan Banks's arrival in Eastvale, Yorkshire, corresponds with a crime wave.

Shannon, Dell. *Case Pending.* 1960

L.A.P.D. Detective Luis Mendoza finds a woman's murder is connected to some unsolved cases.

Treat, Lawrence. *V as in Victim.* 1945

Mitch Taylor and Jub Freeman, detectives of the Twenty-First Precinct, investigate a fatal hit-and-run accident.

Wambaugh, Joseph. *The Blue Knight.* 1972

Officer "Bumper" Wagner has put in twenty years on the force and is just about ready to retire—if he can actually let go.

Wilcox, Collin. *The Lonely Hunter.* 1964

Sergeant Frank Hastings tries to locate his runaway daughter as he tracks a murderer among San Francisco's hippies.

HISTORICAL MYSTERIES

Beck, K. K. *Death in a Deck Chair.* 1984

On her way home after a round-the-world cruise with her wealthy aunt in the 1920s, young Iris Cooper finds herself helping the ship's captain investigate a murder.

Buckley, Fiona. *To Shield the Queen.* 1997

Lady-in-waiting Ursula Blanchard is given the delicate task of protecting Amy Robsart, the wife of Queen Elizabeth I's favorite courtier, who, it is rumored, is being slowly poisoned.

Carr, John Dickson. *Captain Cut-Throat.* 1955

As Napoleon prepares to invade England, Paris police chief Joseph Fouche seeks the help of an English spy to uncover who is behind the Captain Cut-Throat murders.

Chisholm, P. F. *A Famine of Horses.* 1995

Sir Robert Carey escapes the intrigues of the Elizabethan court by becoming the Deputy Warden of the West March, but his arrival at his new post coincides with a murder that could precipitate a civil war between England and Scotland.

Davis, Lindsey. *Silver Pigs.* 1989

In ancient Rome of A.D. 70, private informer Marcus Didius Falco investigates the murder of a senator's niece only to discover the crime has a mysterious connection to some silver mines in Britain.

Day, Dianne. *The Strange Files of Fremont Jones.* 1995

Caroline Fremont Jones escapes an arranged marriage by moving to San Francisco in 1905, where she opens her own typewriting business and becomes involved in intrigue, mystery, and romance.

Doherty, P. C. *Satan in St. Mary's.* 1987

Hugh Corbett, Master of Clerks and Keeper of the Secret Seal, as well as spy for Edward I, is assigned to investigate the suicide of a man who sought sanctuary in a church after killing a moneylender.

Doody, Margaret. *Aristotle Detective.* 1980

When a prominent citizen of 332 B.C. Athens is murdered, a young man seeks the assistance of his mentor, Aristotle, to help prove his cousin is innocent.

King, Laurie. *The Beekeeper's Apprentice.* 1994

Teenager Mary Russell stumbles across a retired beekeeper on the Sussex Downs in 1914, not realizing she has just met the legendary Sherlock Holmes, who is soon to become her mentor in detection.

Lawrence, Margaret. *Hearts and Bones.* 1996

Rutherford, Maine, is still recovering from the recent Revolutionary War when a brutal rape and murder shocks the small town and prompts midwife Hannah Trevor to investigate matters.

Linscott, Gillian. *Sister beneath the Sheet.* 1991

A celebrated courtesan leaves a fortune to a British suffrage group, but when her will is contested, suffragette Nell Bray travels to turn-of-the-century Biarritz to find out if the woman committed suicide or was murdered.

Lovesey, Peter. *Wobble to Death.* 1970

British Sergeant Cribb looks into the murders of contestants who are participating in a Victorian walking race.

Meyers, Maan. *The Dutchman.* 1992

Sheriff Peter Tonneman is determined to find the murderer of his friend before the British invade New Amsterdam in 1664.

Monfredo, Miriam Grace. *Seneca Falls Inheritance.* 1992

Seneca Fall's librarian Glynis Tryon finds herself distracted from preparing for the Women's Rights Convention of 1848 when a woman's body turns up in the canal behind the library.

Newman, Sharan. *Death Comes as Epiphany.* 1993

Catherine LeVendeur, a young novice in a twelfth-century French convent, must track down a manuscript that has disappeared.

Penman, Sharon K. *The Queen's Man.* 1996

Justin de Quincy is entrusted with a letter addressed to Queen Eleanor of Aquitaine only to find he is now ensnared in a deadly mix of politics and danger.

Perry, Anne. *The Cater Street Hangman.* 1979

Charlotte shocks her upper-class Victorian family when she helps Police Inspector Thomas Pitt investigate the murder of a servant.

Peters, Elizabeth. *Crocodile on the Sandbank.* 1975

At a late-nineteenth-century Egyptian dig, spinster Amelia Peabody and archaeologist Radcliffe Emerson team up to solve the mystery of the mummy that wanders their site at night.

Peters, Ellis. *A Morbid Taste for Bones.* 1977

Part of a group of Benedictine monks traveling through medieval England to Wales to acquire the bones of a little-known saint, Brother Cadfael encounters deception and murder along the way.

Robinson, Lynda. *Murder in the Place of Anubis.* 1994

Pharaoh Tutankhamun asks Lord Meren to investigate when a murdered body turns up in the sacred place of Anubis.

Ross, Kate. *Cut to the Quick.* 1993

While staying in the Fontclair's country home for an upcoming wedding, Regency dandy Julian Kestrel finds a murdered woman in his bed.

Rowland, Laura Joh. *Shinju.* 1994

A seventeenth-century Japanese samurai believes a ritual double suicide is really murder and risks everything he has to investigate.

Saylor, Steven. *Roman Blood.* 1991

Roman senator Cicero takes on a client who is accused of murdering his father, but Cicero needs the help of Gordianus the Finder to discover who the real killer is.

Todd, Charles. *A Test of Wills.* 1996

Inspector Ian Rutledge tries to put the voice of a man he was forced to kill during World War I out of his mind as he investigates the murder of a village squire.

van Gulik, Robert Hans. *The Emperor's Pearl.* 1963

Seventh-century Chinese Judge Dee discovers a connection between two murders and the theft of a pearl 100 years earlier.

SUSPENSE

Allegretto, Michael. *Night of Reunion.* 1990

Psychopathic killer Christine Helstrum has unfinished business with Alex Whitaker, and she begins playing a life-and-death game with his family.

Armstrong, Charlotte. *A Dram of Poison.* 1956

A man who considered committing suicide leaves a bottle of poison disguised as olive oil on a bus.

Bloch, Robert. *Psycho.* 1959

Mary Crane's flight to a new life and love is violently interrupted when she stops at the Bates Motel.

Carr, Robyn. *Mind Tryst.* 1992

Divorced lawyer Jackie Sheppard moves to Colorado and meets a handyman whose friendly intentions might just mask a dangerous personality.

Clark, Mary Higgins. *Where Are the Children?* 1983

Nancy Harmon finds herself trapped in a familiar nightmare when her two children from her second marriage disappear, just as her children from her first marriage did years ago.

Davies, Linda. *Nest of Vipers.* 1995

Young, successful currency trader Sarah Jensen goes undercover to find out why a British merchant bank is making more money than it should.

Fielding, Joy. *See Jane Run.* 1991

A woman's deepest instincts tell her something is terribly wrong when she finds $10,000 in her pocket and blood on her clothes but cannot remember her own name.

Frase, H. Michael. *Fatal Gift.* 1996

After witnessing a murder, Kasey Riteman tries to find a way of identifying the killer to the police without revealing her own identity.

Gilstrap, Jonathan. *At All Costs.* 1998

Thirteen-year-old Travis Brighton's folks have always seemed average to him, but Jake and Carolyn Brighton are fugitives who have been falsely accused of a horrible crime.

Harmetz, Aljean. *Off the Face of the Earth.* 1997

When eight-year-old David Greene goes off with a stranger he meets at the mall, his mother and a maverick police officer join forces to find him before it is too late.

Harris, Thomas. *The Silence of the Lambs.* 1988

Because she needs his help, FBI agent Clarice Starling matches wits with psychopathic serial killer Hannibal Lecter in a desperate race to find another murderer.

Heckler, Jonelle. *Final Tour.* 1994

Singer Sass Lindsey is at the height of her career when she decides to retire, but now someone close to her wants to make sure her retirement is permanent.

Highsmith, Patricia. *The Talented Mr. Ripley.* 1955

Tom Ripley finds he likes Dickie Greenleaf's luxurious lifestyle so much that he just might have to take Dickie's place permanently.

Holt, A. J. *Watch Me.* 1995

After stumbling across a computer chat room for serial murders, an FBI agent turns rogue and starts killing the serial killers herself.

Jance, J. A. *Hour of the Hunter.* 1991

A widow and her young son use a Papago grandmother's knowledge of her people's folklore and legends to help defeat a psychotic serial killer.

Mercer, Judy. *Fast Forward.* 1995

Ariel Gold wakes up one morning and after staring in a mirror realizes that she has no idea whose face is looking back at her; she only knows that she is not that woman.

Millar, Margaret. *Beast in View.* 1955

Why does Evelyn Merrick insist that reclusive heiress Helen Clarvoe not only knows her, but owes her as well?

O'Connell, Carol. *Judas Child.* 1998

A diabolically twisted murderer who targets young girls snatches two new victims, but this time his prey are not so easy to kill.

Patterson, James. *Along Came a Spider.* 1993

A Washington, D.C., cop-psychologist and a Secret Service agent work together to stop a gruesome killer who has plans for the two children he kidnapped.

Savage, Tom. *Precipice.* 1994

A beautiful young woman arrives at the Prescott's home in tropical St. Thomas and sets into play a deadly game of deception.

Schneider, Joyce Ann. *Darkness Falls.* 1989

When a psychiatrist discovers similarities between the murder of a patient and her own mother's death twenty years earlier, she begins her own investigation of the crime.

Simpson, Thomas William. *Caretaker.* 1998

Gunn Henderson accepts a new job that includes the use of a company mansion that comes complete with its very own caretaker.

Skillman, Trish Macdonald. *Someone to Watch Over.* 1994

Someone is watching over Kate Eldridge and her two children very carefully, but his concern soon turns into an obsession.

Thompson, Carlene. *The Way You Look Tonight.* 1997

Deborah Robinson begins to wonder if her husband's disappearance could be connected to the horrible killings of several local women.

Wallace, Marilyn. *So Shall You Reap.* 1992

Sarah Hoving discovers someone in her small New England hometown would prefer that old secrets and deadly passions remain hidden.

LEGAL THRILLERS

Bernhardt, William. *Primary Justice.* 1991

Oklahoma attorney Benjamin Kincaid's first case involves helping Jonathan and Bertha Adams adopt a young girl, but when Jonathan is found dead, Benjamin finds himself looking into the murder.

Brandon, Jay. *Fade the Heat.* 1990

Mark Blackwell becomes the target of an unknown enemy when he tries to help clear his son of a rape charge.

Buffa, D. W. *The Defense.* 1997

Defense attorney Joseph Antonelli must decide how far he will go to win a case when he is coerced into defending a man accused of raping a twelve-year-old girl.

Coughlin, William J. *Shadow of a Doubt.* 1991

Charlie Sloan, lawyer and recovering alcoholic, finds himself defending the stepdaughter of a woman he once loved when the girl is charged with murder.

Friedman, Philip. *Reasonable Doubt.* 1990

When his son is murdered, former federal prosecutor Michael Ryan takes on the task of defending his daughter-in-law, who is accused of the crime.

Gardner, Erle Stanley. *The Case of the Velvet Claws.* 1933

A married woman caught up in a blackmail scheme needs Perry Mason's help when her husband is found murdered.

Grisham, John. *The Firm.* 1991

Hired right out of law school by a Memphis law firm, Mitchell McDeere discovers his new employer has ties to organized crime.

Horn, Stephen. *In Her Defense.* 2000

After giving up his high-powered job and his perfect family for a career as a public defender, Frank O'Connell's first client is a glamorous socialite who admits she is guilty of shooting a former secretary of agriculture.

Lashner, William. *Hostile Witness.* 1995

Down-on-his-luck Philadelphia attorney Victor Carl gets the chance of a lifetime when he is invited to become part of a legal team defending a local politician and his aide against a murder charge.

Lescroart, John T. *Hard Evidence.* 1992

When a human hand is found in a shark, Assistant D.A. Dismas Hardy gets involved in one of San Francisco's biggest murder trials.

Margolin, Philip. *After Dark.* 1995

Abigail Griffen, prosecuting attorney and estranged wife of an Oregon Supreme Court judge, is accused of murder when her husband is blown up.

Martini, Steve. *Compelling Evidence.* 1992

An affair with his boss's wife cost defense attorney Paul Madriani his job, but now he must join the defense team when the woman is accused of murdering her spouse.

Meltzer, Brad. *The Tenth Justice.* 1997

Ben Addison, recent law school graduate and new clerk for a U.S. Supreme Court justice, becomes the target of a dangerous blackmailer after he accidentally reveals the outcome of an upcoming case.

O'Shaughnessy, Perri. *Motion to Suppress.* 1997

New to Lake Tahoe, Nina Reilly agrees to help a woman with her divorce only to find the case turning into a murder investigation.

Parker, Barbara. *Suspicion of Innocence.* 1994

When her beautiful, irresponsible sister is found dead, lawyer Gail Conner investigates the "suicide."

Patterson, Richard North. *Degree of Guilt.* 1993

Christopher Paget defends his former wife and lover, Mary Carelli, when she is accused of murdering a famous novelist.

Rosenberg, Nancy Taylor. *Mitigating Circumstances.* 1993

After a criminal invades her home and attacks her daughter, Assistant District Attorney Lily Forrester sets out to exact her own form of revenge.

Scottoline, Lisa. *Rough Justice.* 1997

While waiting for the jury to reach its verdict, Marta Richter's client admits to her he really is guilty of murder, but when Marta tries to find a way to reopen the case, her client tries to find a way to silence his attorney permanently.

Siegel, Barry. *The Perfect Witness.* 1997

Asked to defend an old friend in a murder case, Greg Monarch finds himself bending his own ethical standards to win the case.

Siegel, Sheldon. *Special Circumstances.* 2000

Asked to resign as a partner from his old law firm, Mike Daley opens his own practice and now must defend an old friend and coworker who is accused of murdering two other people at Daley's old firm.

Tannenbaum, Robert K. *No Lesser Plea.* 1987

Assistant District Attorney Roger Karp is determined to keep Mandeville Louis, armed robber and killer, from using the insanity plea to escape prosecution.

Traver, Robert. *Anatomy of a Murder.* 1958

Recently ousted from his job as a D.A., Paul Biegler takes on his replacement in the trial of an army lieutenant accused of murder.

Turow, Scott. *Presumed Innocent.* 1987

Chief Deputy Prosecuting Attorney Rusty Sabich is assigned to investigate the murder of a coworker and former lover.

MEDICAL/BIO THRILLERS

Braver, Gary. *Elixir.* 2000

Chemist Chris Bacon stumbles across a flower in the Papuan rain forest that holds the key to immortality, but he may not live long enough to enjoy the fruits of his research.

Case, John. *The First Horseman.* 1998

Two scientists and a newspaper reporter are caught up in a secretive cult's plans to set loose a plague cultivated from the Spanish flu virus of 1918.

Chiu, Tony. *Positive Match.* 1997

With the help of two computer hackers, a Vietnamese American physician and an investment banker investigate the deadly link between an organ transport company and an HMO.

Christofferson, April. *Clinical Trial.* 2000

Dr. Isabel McLain welcomes the news of a vaccine against the deadly *Hantavirus* but suspects that Native Americans are being endangered in the drug trials.

Cook, Robin. *Coma.* 1977

Medical student Susan Wheeler discovers doctors at Memorial Hospital are harvesting parts from patients sent in for minor surgery and then putting those patients into a coma.

Cordy, Michael. *The Miracle Strain.* 1997

Geneticist Tom Carter becomes convinced that, if he can locate it, a very special strain of DNA can cure his daughter's terminal illness.

Crichton, Michael. *The Andromeda Strain.* 1969

When an unmanned satellite returns to Earth bearing unknown but lethal microorganisms, a dangerous epidemic breaks out.

Cuthbert, Margaret. *The Silent Cradle.* 1998

A series of deadly incidents occurring during otherwise routine baby deliveries causes OB-GYN Rae Murphy to investigate.

Dantz, William R. *The Seventh Sleeper.* 1991

When comatose people, dubbed "sleepers," begin to appear in Miami ghettos, Sara Copley, of the Public Health Department, suspects they are victims of a sinister new "designer" drug.

Dreyer, Eileen. *Bad Medicine.* 1995

Trauma nurse Molly Burke gradually realizes that some people will do anything to keep her from investigating a strange increase in suicide deaths among local lawyers.

Ferguson, Tom. *No Deadly Drug.* 1968

Physician Gabe Austin discovers a new wonder drug, manufactured by the company his new girlfriend works for, has unexpected and frightening side effects.

Gerritsen, Tess. *Harvest.* 1996

Boston Bayside Hospital surgical resident Abby DiMatteo ends up risking her career and her life when she tries to shut down an organ-harvesting network with ties to the former Soviet Union.

Hogan, Chuck. *The Blood Artists.* 1998

Two scientists, once friends but now bitter enemies, must work together to locate the only woman in the world whose blood holds immunities to a vicious virus.

Lynch, Patrick. *Carriers.* 1995

A team of U.S. biological warfare experts is sent to the jungles of Sumatra to locate the source of an Ebola-like virus.

Marr, John S. *The Eleventh Plague.* 1998

Virologist Jack Byrne tries to stop a mad scientist from successfully setting loose the ten plagues of the Bible plus one nasty additional one.

Mezrich, Ben. *Fertile Ground.* 1999

Fertility expert Jack Foster makes a terrifying discovery that may explain why Boston suffers from the highest infertility rate in the nation.

Miller, Timothy. *Practice to Deceive.* 1991

Plastic surgeon Lionel Stern will do whatever it takes to prove sloppy, incompetent plastic surgeon Morris Gold is murdering his patients.

Ouellette, Pierre. *The Third Pandemic.* 1996

Scientist Elaine Wilkes is the only person in the world who knows which drug will successfully treat a terrifying bacteria that appears to be resistant to all known antibiotics.

Palmer, Michael. *Critical Judgment.* 1996

Emergency room doctor Abbey Dolan grows increasingly concerned about the number of patients with serious but mysteriously unidentifiable medical problems in her small town.

Pottinger, Stanley. *The Fourth Procedure.* 1995

Determined to end back-alley abortions, Congressman Jack MacLeod and pioneering physician Rachel Redpath are concerned when strangely mutilated bodies begin to appear at the D.C. medical examiner's office.

Preston, Richard. *The Cobra Event.* 1997

Alice Austen, a Centers for Disease Control doctor, finds herself up against a madman who has unleashed a deadly new virus on New York City.

Scott, Holden. *The Carrier.* 2000

A brilliant Harvard student discovers a cure for cancer only to find himself pitted against his mentor and the FBI.

Shobin, David. *The Provider.* 2000

A dedicated young doctor is determined to uncover the sinister conspiracy of silence surrounding a rash of mysterious neonatal deaths.

Wilson, F. Paul. *The Select.* 1995

The Ingraham Medical School offers exceptional medical training free of charge, but new student Quinn Clearu discovers the hidden costs of attending this prestigious school.

Wydra, Frank. *The Cure.* 1992

Researcher Luke Chinsky and journalist Brenda Byrne find out that a drug cartel will do anything, up to and including murder, to keep a cure for AIDS off the market.

ROMANTIC SUSPENSE

Aiken, Joan. *Blackground.* 1989

After being swept up in a whirlwind marriage to a handsome millionaire, actress Cat Conwil suddenly starts to remember things about her new husband.

Brown, Sandra. *French Silk.* 1992

Claire Laurent, owner of a mail-order lingerie company, is the prime suspect in the murder of a TV evangelist.

du Maurier, Daphne. *Rebecca.* 1938

The second Mrs. de Winter discovers that even though her husband's first wife, Rebecca, is dead, her legacy lingers on at Manderley.

Eberhart, Mignon G. *The House on the Roof.* 1935

Deborah Cavert suspects she is being framed for the murder of diva Mary Monroe.

Forster, Suzanne. *Every Breath She Takes.* 1999

When a killer begins targeting stalkers, Los Angeles Police Detective Rio Walker turns to stalking expert Carlie Bishop for help only to wonder if Carlie might not be the killer herself.

Gardner, Lisa. *The Perfect Husband.* 1998

When her husband, who has killed ten women, escapes and comes looking for her, Tess Beckett turns to a burned-out ex-marine to teach her how to fight back.

Hinze, Vicki. *Duplicity.* 1999

Captain Tracy Keener risks both her reputation and her life when she refuses to stop looking into the case of a fellow officer accused of treason and murder.

Hooper, Kay. *Amanda.* 1995

A woman comes forward claiming to be missing heiress Amanda Daulton, but someone is determined that the new Amanda will never get her share of the family fortune.

Howard, Linda. *All the Queen's Men.* 1999

CIA agent John Medina needs the help of electronics expert Niema Burdock, whose husband was tragically killed on an earlier mission with Medina, to trap a ruthless arms dealer.

Johansen, Iris. *Ugly Duckling.* 1996

After surviving a brutal attack that left her husband and young daughter dead, plain Nell Calder is transformed through plastic surgery into a beautiful woman determined to find the person responsible for killing her family.

Johnston, Velda. *Flight to Yesterday.* 1990

Sara Hargreaves discovers her only hope of freedom lies in uncovering the truth about who killed plastic surgeon Manuelo Covarrubias.

Kaye, M. M. *Death in Zanzibar.* 1983

After arriving at her family's place in Zanzibar, Dany Ashton discovers someone among the guests staying at the House of Shade is a cunning murderer.

Krentz, Jayne Ann. *Sharp Edges.* 1998

Museum curator Eugenia Swift and private investigator Cyrus Chandler Colfax must work together to find the person responsible for the death of a famous glass collector.

Lee, Rachel. *After I Dream.* 2000

Former Navy SEAL and deep-sea-diver Chase Mattingly reluctantly helps psychologist Callie Carlson when her brother is accused of murdering two fishermen.

Llewellyn, Caroline. *The Masks of Rome.* 1988

Arriving in Rome during the Carnival season to restore the Torreleone family paintings, Kate Roy finds herself caught up in a web of corruption and deceit.

Lowell, Elizabeth. *Amber Beach.* 1997

Honor Donovan hires Jake Mallory to help her locate her missing brother, who disappeared somewhere in the Puget Sound, along with a fortune in amber.

Michaels, Barbara. *Wait for What Will Come.* 1978

Carla Tregellas arrives at the mansion she has inherited on the coast of Cornwall only to be warned to leave at once or become another victim of her family's curse.

Rinehart, Mary Roberts. *The Circular Staircase.* 1908

Spinster Rachel Innes rents a house for the summer and becomes convinced the place is haunted when a murderer strikes.

Robards, Karen. *Hunter's Moon.* 1995

After she is caught trying to take the money the FBI left as bait, horse-groomer Molly Ballard finds herself involved in an FBI investigation into a horse-race-fixing scheme.

Roberts, Nora. *Hidden Riches.* 1994

Antiques dealer Dora Conroy purchases something at an auction meant for someone else and becomes the target of a vengeful killer.

Seeley, Mabel. *The Beckoning Door.* 1950

When the cousin who broke up her romance and inherited the family estate is found dead, Cathy Kingman must find the real murderer in order to prove her own innocence.

Stewart, Mary. *Airs above the Ground.* 1965

When her husband appears in a newsreel shot in Vienna, after he supposedly left for a business trip in Stockholm, Vanessa March knows something is wrong.

Stuart, Anne. *Shadow Lover.* 1999

Carolyn Smith wonders how Alex MacDowell could return home because Carolyn is positive she saw the real Alex murdered eighteen years earlier.

Whitney, Phyllis A. *Emerald.* 1983

Journalist Carol Hamilton finds danger and romance in Palm Springs when she attempts to discover the reason her glamorous great-aunt gave up her movie career.

Woods, Sherryl. *Twilight.* 1997

Dana Miller travels to the last place her husband was seen alive in an effort to locate his killer only to find herself falling in love with the man she holds responsible for his death.

ACTION AND ADVENTURE

Bagley, Desmond. *The Golden Keel.* 1963

South African boat-builder Peter Halloran searches for a way to recover Mussolini's lost treasure.

Cornwell, Bernard. *Sharpe's Rifles: Richard Sharpe and the French Invasion of Galicia, January 1809.* 1988

While retreating from Napoleon's forces in Spain, Richard Sharpe must take charge of a group of Rifles who are cut off from the British army.

Cussler, Clive. *Raise the Titanic.* 1976

Dirk Pitt battles the Soviets for a rare cache of byzanium believed to be somewhere on the sunken *Titanic.*

Davidson, Lionel. *The Rose of Tibet.* 1962

Charles Houston goes in search of his missing brother, last seen in the remote mountains of Tibet.

Easterman, Daniel. *The Ninth Buddha.* 1989

When his young son is kidnapped, former British intelligence agent Christopher Wylam begins a desperate search that leads him to a Buddhist monastery.

Forster, C. S. *Mr. Midshipman Hornblower.* 1950

During the 1790s, seventeen-year-old Horatio Hornblower begins his rise through the ranks of the British navy.

Garrison, Paul. *Fire and Ice.* 1998

Michael Stone tries to rescue his wife and young daughter, who have been kidnapped by the owner of a giant tanker.

Griffin, W. E. B. *The Lieutenants.* 1982

World War II turns a group of American boys into soldiers.

Haggard, H. Rider. *King Solomon's Mines.* 1885

Allan Quatermain, Henry Curtis, and John Good set out for the darkest depths of Africa in search of Henry's missing brother and the fabled diamond mines of Solomon.

Higgins, Jack. *Night of the Fox.* 1987

Three imposters join forces in a daring and dangerous mission to rescue a wounded American soldier who has washed ashore on the German occupied island of Jersey.

Innes, Hammond. *Blue Ice.* 1948

Mineral expert Bill Gansert searches Norway for a man who disappeared there ten years earlier.

Llewellyn, Sam. *Sea Story.* 1988

A group of men and women compete against each other to win the Great Circle sailing race around the world.

MacLean, Alistair. *The Guns of Navarone.* 1957

A small band of British commandos must infiltrate a German-held Greek island and destroy the guns of Navarone.

Marcinko, Richard. *Rogue Warrior II: Red Cell.* 1994

Dick Marcinko and his team of Red Cell SEALs try to keep American nuclear weapons out of the hands of the Japanese and North Koreans.

Preston, Douglas J., and Lincoln Child. *Riptide.* 1998

Martin Hatch joins an expedition searching Ragged Island for the legendary treasure of pirate Edward Ockham.

Reeves-Stevens, Judith, and Garfield Reeves-Stevens. *Icefire.* 1998

Navy SEAL Captain Mitch Webber and oceanographer Cory Rey try to stop a tidal wave created by a group of insurgent Chinese who set off nuclear warheads in Antarctica.

Reilly, Matthew J. *Ice Station.* 1999

Lieutenant Shane "Scarecrow" Schofield leads a group of U.S. Marines on a rescue mission after scientists discover something strange deep beneath Wilkes Ice Station in Antarctica.

Sabatini, Rafael. *The Sea Hawk.* 1915

An English gentleman falsely accused of murder becomes a Barbary pirate.

Smith, Wilbur. *The Seventh Scroll.* 1995

A beautiful Egyptologist and an English adventurer risk their lives to locate the whereabouts of a pharaoh's tomb.

Stevenson, Robert Louis, III. *Torchlight.* 1997

The CIA sends two former U.S. Navy divers on a covert mission to infiltrate an international arms dealer's expedition to retrieve a billion dollars in sunken gold.

Woods, Stuart. *White Cargo.* 1988

Millionaire Wendell Catledge goes after the Colombian drug lord who murdered his wife and kidnapped his daughter.

Wren, P. C. *Beau Geste.* 1927

Three English brothers join the French Foreign Legion after a family jewel disappears.

TECHNO-THRILLERS

Ballard, Robert. *Bright Shark.* 1992

Governments on two continents risk an armed showdown after the U.S. Navy finds the remains of an Israeli submarine, which had vanished twenty years earlier.

Berent, Mark. *Rolling Thunder.* 1989

Three U.S. Air Force pilots face the early years of the Vietnamese War together.

Bond, Larry K. *Red Phoenix.* 1990

Armed with Soviet weapons, North Korea invades South Korea, setting off the second Korean War.

Brown, Dale. *Fatal Terrain.* 1997

When the People's Republic of China strikes out at Taiwan, it is up to aerial strike warfare expert Patrick McLanahan to save the day.

Buff, Joe. *Deep Sound Channel.* 2000

In 2011, World War III has begun, and U.S. Lieutenant Commander Jeffrey Fuller's mission is to destroy a South African lab reputed to be cooking up the ultimate biological weapon.

Clancy, Tom. *The Hunt for Red October.* 1984

Both the Russians and the Americans chase a runaway top secret Russian missile submarine around the Atlantic Ocean.

Cobb, James H. *Choosers of the Slain.* 1996

In 2006, U.S. Commander Amanda Garrett and her high-tech stealth destroyer are Antarctica's sole protection when Argentina invades.

Coonts, Stephen. *Flight of the Intruder.* 1986

Looking for honor and glory, Jake "Cool Hand" Grafton, along with a renegade bombardier named Tiger, flies his A-6 Intruder jet deep into North Vietnam on one last mission.

Coyle, Harold W. *Code of Honor.* 1994

General Scott Discon and Captain Nancy Kozak lead U.S. troops into Colombia on a peacekeeping mission that turns into a full-scale war.

DiMercurio, Michael. *Attack of the Sea Wolf.* 1993

The captain of a state-of-the-art U.S. nuclear submarine comes to the rescue when Chinese forces capture the USS *Tampa.*

Franklet, Duane. *Bad Memory.* 1997

A troubleshooter and the CEO for the world's largest personal computer manufacturer confront a ruthless and resourceful hacker who demands a payoff to leave the company alone.

Gribble, Joe. L. *Silent Lightning.* 1998

Colonel "Ironman" Jones and a team of experts are out to destroy Syria's newest weapon: an airborne laser-guided missile system.

Hagberg, David. *High Flight.* 1995

A former CIA field officer is hired by an airline company to investigate several recent accidents.

Harrison, Payne. *Forbidden Summit.* 1997

Intelligence officer Frank Hannon investigates the lack of response by government officials when four unidentified aircraft are sighted descending over North America.

Herman, Richard. *The Warbirds.* 1989

Colonel Anthony "Muddy" Waters whips a band of ne'er-do-well flyers into a crack team capable of flying the mighty F-4 Phantom jets.

Ing, Dean. *The Ransom of Black Stealth One.* 1989

A man the CIA supposedly killed years ago steals the most sophisticated and dangerous aircraft ever designed by the Americans.

Joseph, Mark. *Typhoon.* 1991

Deep beneath the Arctic Ocean the world's most sophisticated and powerful submarines engage in a deadly game of deception.

Pineiro, R. J. *01-01-00: The Novel of the Millennium.* 1999

An FBI analyst and an anthropologist think the code hidden in a computer virus might be linked to an ancient Mayan prophecy.

Robinson, Patrick. *Nimitz Class.* 1997

After an aircraft carrier is lost in an apparent nuclear accident, U.S. Naval Intelligence investigates and finds out a rogue submarine armed with nuclear weapons may have been responsible.

Stewart, Chris. *Shattered Bone.* 1997

The Ukraine activates an undercover agent in the United States who hijacks a B-1B bomber loaded with nuclear weapons.

ESPIONAGE FICTION

Allbeury, Ted. *The Judas Factor.* 1984

SIS agent Tad Anders must kidnap an East German KGB agent who is killing British operatives.

Altman, John. *A Gathering of Spies.* 2000

A British MI-5 agent is the only one who can stop a female Nazi agent carrying secrets from Los Alamos.

Ambler, Eric. *A Coffin for Dimitrios.* 1939

An English mystery writer attempts to trace the path of a Greek spy found dead in Istanbul.

Anthony, Evelyn. *The Defector.* 1981

A beautiful British agent finds herself falling in love with a KGB defector.

Armstrong, Campbell. *Jig.* 1987

British counterterror specialist Inspector Pagon tracks the IRA's top assassin.

Buchan, John. *The Thirty-Nine Steps.* 1915

Mining engineer Richard Hannay stumbles across an assassination plot that could trigger a war between Germany and England.

Deighton, Len. *The Ipcress File.* 1964

A British secret service agent looks into the disappearance of a biochemist.

DeMille, Nelson. *The Charm School.* 1988

A young American on vacation in the Soviet Union stumbles across a secret camp where Russians are being taught how to imitate Americans.

Fleming, Ian. *Casino Royale.* 1954

James Bond, Agent 007, attempts to break the bank of Le Chiffre and smash the Soviet murder organization SMERSH.

Follett, Ken. *The Eye of the Needle.* 1978

One woman tries to stop a Nazi agent attempting to escape England with the secret of D day.

Freemantle, Brian. *Charlie M.* 1977

SIS agent Charlie Muffin is put in charge of things when the head of the KGB attempts to defect.

Furst, Alan. *Night Soldiers.* 1988

Bulgarian Khristo Stoianev becomes an agent for the NKVD who put him to work during the Spanish civil war, but after Khristo feels betrayed, he turns against his employers.

Gilman, Dorothy. *The Unexpected Mrs. Pollifax.* 1966

Sixtysomething widow Emily Pollifax wants more out of life than her gardening club can provide, so she becomes a courier for the CIA.

Hall, Adam. *The Quiller Memorandum.* 1965

British agent Quiller's latest assignment is to locate a dangerous group of ex-Nazis in Berlin.

Hartov, Steven. *The Devil's Shepherd.* 2000

Two Israeli intelligence agents must rescue a Czech defector in Ethiopia who knows the identity of the mole who has infiltrated Israel's nuclear defense system.

Houghan, Jim. *Kingdom Come.* 2000

A CIA agent's life is in danger when he uncovers a sinister plot involving his employers.

Household, Geoffrey. *The Rogue Male.* 1939

An English hunter sets his gun sights on a European dictator only to become the quarry himself.

le Carré, John. *The Spy Who Came In from the Cold.* 1964

British agent Alex Leamas is given one last assignment before he retires: play an agent defecting to the East Germans.

Ludlum, Robert. *The Aquitaine Progression.* 1984

American lawyer Joel Converse becomes involved in a terrifying conspiracy masterminded by a group bent on resurrecting the Fourth Reich.

Lynds, Gayle. *Masquerade.* 1996

A woman with amnesia is told she is a top intelligence agent only to later discover that the people she is supposed to trust are trying to kill her.

MacInnes, Helen. *Above Suspicion.* 1954

While on vacation in Europe, an Oxford professor and his wife search for an anti-Nazi agent.

Mathews, Francine. *The Cutout.* 2001

CIA analyst Caroline Carmichael thought her husband died in an airplane crash, but then he is spotted in Berlin at the same time the U.S. vice president is kidnapped by a terrorist group.

Morrell, David. *The Brotherhood of the Rose.* 1984

A mysterious man raises two orphans, turning them into intelligence operatives and assassins.

O'Donnell, Peter. *Modesty Blaise.* 1965

Modesty, a stunning ex-mobster, is recruited by British intelligence to take on a villain who is stirring up trouble in the Middle East.

Price, Anthony. *The Labyrinth Makers.* 1971

A British agent is assigned to find out why the Soviets are so interested in a World War II plane that has recently been recovered from a lake.

Reiss, Bob. *The Last Spy.* 1993

Soviet spies who have successfully set themselves up with new lives in America find themselves in trouble when the Soviet Union collapses.

Tan, Maureen. *AKA Jane.* 1997

Ready to retire to a life as a mystery writer, burned-out British MI-5 agent Jane Nichols plunges into one last mission when she crosses paths with an old nemesis in Savannah.

TRUE CRIME

Alexander, Shana. *Nutcracker: Money, Madness, and Murder: A Family Album.* 1985

A twisted, evil mother convinces her two sons to murder their wealthy grandfather.

Arax, Max. *In My Father's Name: A Family, a Town, a Murder.* 1996

L.A. Times investigative reporter Arax attempts to solve a crime that destroyed his childhood: the murder of his father, who was killed by two gunmen in 1972 in what appeared to be a mob "hit."

Baden, Michael M., with Judith Adler Hennessee. *Unnatural Death: Confessions of a Medical Examiner.* 1992

A former forensic pathologist and New York City medical examiner reviews several cases while explaining how medical examiners work.

Behn, Noel. *Lindbergh: The Crime.* 1994

A new look at the famous kidnapping and murder case that proposes the killer was closer to the crime than anyone ever suspected.

Bledsoe, Jerry. *Before He Wakes: A True Story of Money, Marriage, Sex, and Murder.* 1994

Beneath the surface of a picture-perfect North Carolina wife and mother lies the mind of a cunning, cold-blooded killer.

Bommersbach, Jana. *The Trunk Murderess: Winnie Ruth Judd.* 1992

A journalist exonerates the Arizona woman known as "The Trunk Murderess" who spent thirty-nine years in prison for shooting, dismembering, and stuffing into trunks the bodies of her two best friends.

Breo, Dennis L. *The Crime of the Century: Richard Speck and the Murder of Eight Student Nurses.* 1993

A Texas drifter named Richard Speck brutally murders eight student nurses in Chicago in 1966.

Bugliosi, Vincent. *Helter Skelter: The True Story of the Manson Murders.* 1974

The district attorney who prosecuted the Manson family recounts the story of the psychotic Charles, his followers, and their trial and punishment for the murders that shocked Hollywood in 1969.

Capote, Truman. *In Cold Blood: A True Account of a Multiple Murder and Its Consequences.* 1965

The 1959 murder of a Kansas farm family shocked the country and prompted a celebrated novelist to write about the capture, trial, and execution of the killers.

Carlo, Phillip. *The Night Stalker: The True Story of America's Most Feared Serial Killer.* 1996

Using death-row interviews, the author narrates the life of serial murderer Richard Ramirez, from his youthful brushes with the law to his killing spree that terrorized Los Angeles.

D'Amato, Barbara. *The Doctor, the Murder, the Mystery: The True Story of the Dr. John Banion Murder Case.* 1992

A Chicago physician who is found guilty of murdering his wife in 1968 finally proves his innocence seven years later.

Douglas, John E., and Mark Olshaker. *The Anatomy of Motive: The FBI's Legendary Mindhunter Explores the Key to Understanding and Catching Violent Criminals.* 1999

An FBI agent who is an authority on the subject of criminal profiling attempts to explain what motivates serial, mass, and spree killers.

Ellroy, James. *My Dark Places.* 1996

A mystery writer obsessed with his mother's murder in 1958 probes her killing, its impact on his life, and the results of the murder investigation.

Firstman, Richard, and Jamie Talan. *The Death of Innocents: A True Story of Murder, Medicine, and High-Stakes Science.* 1997

The suspicious deaths of several children in one household, earlier attributed to sudden infant death syndrome (SIDS), are investigated years later and found to have been the result of Munchausen syndrome by proxy.

Gibson, Gregory. *Gone Boy: A Walkabout.* 1999

Gregory Gibson sets out on an odyssey to understand what happened after his bright, talented eighteen-year-old son becomes one of the victims of a murderous rampage at Simons Rock College in Massachusetts.

Herzog, Arthur. *The Woodchipper Murder.* 1989

The disappearance of Helle Craft in 1986 was considered to be a routine missing person case until a local private investigator proved otherwise.

Higdon, Hal. *Crime of the Century: The Leopold and Loeb Case.* 1975

The murder of young Bobby Franks in 1924 by two Chicago students shocked the city and the nation by its senseless brutality.

Lardner, George, Jr. *The Stalking of Kristin: A Father Investigates the Murder of His Daughter.* 1995

A Pulitzer Prize–winning investigative journalist describes how the law could not protect his young daughter from being murdered by her jealous boyfriend.

McGinniss, Joe. *Fatal Vision.* 1983

Dr. Jeffrey MacDonald was convicted of murdering his wife and two young daughters in 1979 but always maintained his innocence.

Olsen, Jack. *Son: A Psychopath and His Victims.* 1983

A serial rapist's relationship with his vicious and manipulative mother may be the key to the crimes he committed.

Robins, Natalie, and Steven M. Aronson. *Savage Grace.* 1985

The saga of the wealthy, powerful Baekeland family, who seemed to have it all until great-grandson Tony murdered his mother in 1972.

Rule, Ann. *The Stranger beside Me.* 1980

A former policewoman discovers that charming Ted Bundy, who worked with her in a Seattle crisis clinic, is really a convicted killer of three young woman and self-confessed murderer of at least thirty-five more.

Sebold, Alice. *Lucky.* 1999

> The author documents her horrific experience of being raped as a college student and the trial that followed.

Thernstrom, Melanie. *Halfway to Heaven: Diary of a Harvard Murder.* 1997

> Trang Phuong Ho achieved the American dream of attending Harvard University only to be murdered by her roommate, whose bizarre behavior and cries for help went unnoticed.

Thompson, Thomas. *Blood and Money.* 1976

> A Houston surgeon murders his socialite wife and then is murdered himself a few years later.

SHORT STORY ANTHOLOGIES

Adrian, Jack, and Robert Adey, eds. *Murder Impossible: An Extravaganza of Miraculous Murders, Fantastic Felonies, and Incredible Criminals.* 1990

> A collection of "locked room" murders and other impossible crimes by well-known authors like Edgar Wallace and John Dickson Carr.

Alfred Hitchcock Presents My Favorites in Suspense. 1959

> A hefty anthology introduced by the master that includes the eponymously named story by Daphne du Maurier that was the basis for Alfred Hitchcock's film *The Birds*.

Block, Lawrence, ed. *Death Cruise: Crime Stories in the Open Seas.* 1999

> All the mystery stories in this collection have a seagoing theme.

Block, Lawrence, ed. *Master's Choice: Mystery Stories by Today's Top Writers and the Masters Who Inspired Them.* 1999

> Each story, written by a current popular author, includes the story that inspired him or her.

Douglas, Carole Nelson, ed. *Midnight Louie's Pet Detectives.* 1998

> Douglas's feline sleuth, Midnight Louie, presents a menagerie of mysteries featuring animals.

Haining, Peter, ed. *Murder on the Menu.* 1991

A feast of culinary-themed mystery stories.

Heald, Tim, ed. *A Classic English Crime.* 1990

An homage to the mistress of traditional mysteries, Agatha Christie, these thirteen stories were written to commemorate the 100th anniversary of her birth by members of the British Crime Writers Association.

Hillerman, Tony, ed. *The Best American Mystery Stories of the Century.* 2000

The crème de la crème of stories, written by a selection of authors that spans the twentieth century.

Hillerman, Tony, ed. *The Mysterious West.* 1994

A collection of stories by authors such as Bill Crider and J. A. Jance that feature the mysterious culture and terrain of the West.

Hollywood Kills. 1993

Glamorous, yet deadly, Hollywood is the focus for this compilation of stories from such authors as Robert Bloch and Ron Goulart.

Hutchings, Janet, ed. *Simply the Best Mysteries: Edgar Award Winners and Front-Runners.* 1998

A selection of stories that either won the Mystery Writers of America Best Short Story Edgar or were runners-up.

Malice Domestic One: An Anthology of Original Traditional Mystery Stories. 1992

The first in an annual offering of traditional mystery stories that has now reached volume 10.

Manson, Cynthia, ed. *Murder by the Book: Literary Mysteries from "Alfred Hitchcock's Mystery Magazine" and "Ellery Queen's Mystery Magazine."* 1995

The stories in this anthology originally appeared in these two popular mystery magazines and all feature a bookish or literary aspect.

Manson, Cynthia, ed. *Murder to Music: Musical Mysteries from "Ellery Queen's Mystery Magazine" and "Alfred Hitchcock's Mystery Magazine."* 1997

Stories by authors including Cornell Woolrich and George Baxt all feature a musical theme and are sure to strike a chord.

Mary Higgins Clark Presents "The Plot Thickens." 1997

Write a mystery story that includes a thick fog, a thick book, and a thick steak? Eleven authors rose to the challenge, including Janet Evanovitch and Edna Buchanan.

Muller, Marcia, and Bill Pronzini, eds. *Detective Duos.* 1997

The stories here showcase crime-solving twosomes, including Francis Lockridge and Richard Lockridge's Pam and Jerry North and Michael Gilbert's Mr. Calder and Mr. Behrens.

Paretsky, Sara, ed. *A Woman's Eye.* 1991

Female crime writers are the focus of this collection of twenty-one short mystery stories.

Randisi, Robert J., ed. *The Eyes Have It: The First Private Eye Writers of America Anthology.* 1984

Shamuses of all shapes and sizes are showcased in this first Private Eye Writers of America anthology.

Randisi, Robert J., ed. *First Cases: First Appearances of Classic Private Eyes.* 1996

This compilation of stories presents the early cases of series detectives, such as Sue Grafton's Kinsey Millhone and Jeremiah Healy's John Francis Cuddy.

Raphael, Lawrence W., ed. *Mystery Midrash: An Anthology of Jewish Mystery and Detective Fiction.* 1999

An anthology of Jewish-themed mystery and detective stories, which includes ones by Faye Kellerman and Stuart M. Kaminsky.

Slung, Michelle, ed. *Murder for Halloween: Tales of Suspense.* 1994

The scariest holiday of the year is the springboard for a collection of mysterious tales.

Spillane, Mickey, and Max Allan Collins, eds. *Murder Is My Business.* 1994

A short story collection focusing on criminals whose business is murder for hire.

Wallace, Marilyn, ed. *The Best of Sisters in Crime.* 1997

These stories have been selected from the annual Sisters in Crime anthologies.

Westlake, Donald, ed. *Murderous Schemes: An Anthology of Classic Detective Stories.* 1996

Classic British and American mysteries are presented as illustrations of eight different mystery canons, including "The Armchair Detective" and "The Caper."

Woods, Paula L., ed. *Spooks, Spies, and Private Eyes: Black Mystery, Crime, and Suspense Fiction of the Twentieth Century.* 1995

A collection of short mystery fiction featuring past and present black detectives, much of which has long been unavailable to readers.

GENREBLENDED MYSTERIES

Ambrose, David. *Superstition.* 1998

A university professor gathers together a group with the intent of "creating a ghost," but they find their project may be more successful than they imagined when their ghost starts killing off members of the group.

Becker, Walter. *Link.* 1998

Paleoanthropologist Samantha Colby discovers the "missing link" that will fill in the gaps of human evolution, but she needs help to keep the artifact out of the hands of several unscrupulous competitors.

Benson, Ann. *The Plague Tales.* 1997

A fourteenth-century physician caught performing an autopsy runs for his life across plague-infested Europe; at the same time, in the twenty-first century, a medical archaeologist unknowingly sets loose the bubonic plague.

Bradley, Marion Zimmer. *Ghostlight.* 1995

While researching information for a book on her celebrity father, occultist Thorne Blackburn, parapsychologist Truth Jourdemayne becomes involved with a group bent on resurrecting Blackburn's work.

Butcher, Jim. *Storm Front.* 2000

The Chicago Police Department hire wizard Harry Dresden as a consultant for their latest case: a couple found brutally murdered by magical means.

Carroll, Jerry Jay. *Inhuman Beings.* 1998

A wealthy psychic who insists that aliens are about to take over the United States of America hires private eye Goodwin Armstrong to help her find proof that will convince others of the threat.

Crichton, Michael. *Jurassic Park.* 1990

A group of people is stranded on an island off Costa Rica where genetically cloned dinosaurs are running wild.

Darton, John. *Neanderthal.* 1996

Matt Mattison and Susan Arnot, former lovers and now academic rivals, are sent to investigate the disappearance of a Harvard paleontologist in Tajikistan.

Dietrich, William. *Getting Back.* 2000

In the middle of the twenty-first century, a computer programmer joins a group of adventurers who are dropped into the middle of a now-deserted Australia.

Garcia, Eric. *Anonymous Rex.* 1999

Down on his luck Los Angeles private detective Vincent Rubio, who is actually a dinosaur in disguise (and not the only one), investigates the murder of his partner.

Garrett, Randall. *Too Many Magicians.* 1966

Magic is science in an alternate world England, and forensic sorcerer Sean O'Lochlainn works with royal Investigator-in-Chief Lord Darcy to solve mysteries.

Hambly, Barbara. *Those Who Hunt the Night.* 1988

Professor James Asher is coerced into investigating who is killing vampires in Edwardian London.

Huff, Tanya. *Blood Price.* 1991

An ex-cop turned private investigator must team up with a romance-writing vampire to stop a grisly killer.

Jackson, Shirley. *The Haunting of Hill House.* 1959

Hill House's reputation of inexplicable phenomena does not deter four people from gathering there for a psychic experiment.

James, Donald. *Monstrum.* 1997

In civil-war-torn twenty-first-century Russia, Police Inspector Constantine Vadim is transferred to Moscow, where his first case involves a serial killer, popularly known as *the monstrum,* who targets young women.

Klavan, Andrew. *The Uncanny.* 1998

A young Hollywood producer, famous for his horror films, comes to England looking for a real ghost story.

Long, Jeff. *The Descent.* 1999

While leading a group on a climb in Tibet, mountaineer Ike Crockett discovers hell may really exist, and its inhabitants are not happy about being disturbed.

Macardle, Dorothy. *The Uninvited.* 1942

A brother and sister discover their bargain-priced Devonshire home is haunted by a past evil.

Neville, Katherine. *The Eight.* 1988

An eighteenth-century French nun and a twentieth-century computer expert both become caught up in the search for a chess set once owned by Charlemagne that reportedly is the key to great power.

Preston, Douglas J., and Lincoln Child. *Relic.* 1995

An FBI agent, a journalist, and a graduate student try to stop a monster from the Amazon who is running loose in the basement of New York City's Museum of Natural History.

Robb, J. D. *Naked in Death.* 1995

In 2058, N.Y.P.D. Lieutenant Eve Dallas investigates a series of murders and finds herself fighting her attraction to her chief suspect, a mysterious billionaire.

Rovin, Jeff. *Vespers.* 1998

A brave cop and a beautiful zoologist join forces to battle billions of bats that are attacking people and swarming toward New York City.

Smith, Michael Marshall. *Spares.* 1997

After spending five years guarding human "spares" on a corporate farm, Jack Randall becomes so angry at their treatment that he helps seven of the inmates escape only to find that someone will stop at nothing to get his property back.

Vitola, Denise. *Quantum Moon.* 1996

Twenty-first-century District Marshal Ty Merrick must find out who murdered a powerful district councilman's wife while finding a way to keep the government from finding out about her own problem with lycanthropy.

B

Mystery Book Lists by Theme

CLASSIC MYSTERIES

Aird, Catherine. *The Religious Body*. 1966

The murder of a nun sends Inspector C. D. Sloan to the convent of St. Anselm searching for a killer.

Allingham, Margery. *The Black Dudley Murder*. 1930

Albert Campion finds out a weekend in the country can be murder.

Brand, Christianna. *Heads You Lose*. 1942

Inspector Cockrill is on the trail of a killer who hates women.

Carr, John Dickson. *Hag's Nook*. 1933

Gideon Fell investigates when the latest Starbeth male is found dead after spending time at Hag's Nook, the old gallows at an abandoned prison.

Chesterton, G. K. *The Innocence of Father Brown*. 1911

Unassuming Father Brown solves a variety of crimes by putting himself in the mind of the criminal.

Christie, Agatha. *The Mysterious Affair at Styles*. 1921

Belgian war refugee Hercule Poirot investigates the murder of the wealthy mistress of Styles Court, who is found poisoned in her locked bedroom.

Crispin, Edmund. *The Case of the Gilded Fly.* 1944

Oxford professor Gervase Fen ends up in the middle of a murder investigation when the leading lady of a theatrical troupe is killed.

Daly, Elizabeth. *Unexpected Night.* 1940

When a young man dies after inheriting millions, rare book and autograph expert Henry Gamadge wonders if it was an accidental death or murder.

Doyle, Sir Arthur Conan. *A Study in Scarlet.* 1888

Sherlock Holmes and his collaborator Dr. Watson meet in their first case, which features a corpse with no wounds and a mysterious phrase drawn in blood.

Innes, Michael. *Death at the President's Lodging.* 1936

The president of an old English university is murdered, and Inspector John Appleby looks for the killer amidst the inhabitants of the college.

Lathen, Emma. *Banking on Death.* 1961

A missing heir winds up dead, and banker John Putnam Thatcher hopes to find the solution to his murder somewhere in the textile industry.

Lockridge, Richard, and Francis Lockridge. *The Norths Meet Murder.* 1940

While working out the arrangements for a party, Pam and Jerry North discover a corpse in the empty apartment above theirs.

MacDonald, John D. *Deep Blue Goodbye.* 1964

Travis McGee, self-described "retriever of valuables," agrees to help Cathy Kerr get back her late father's treasure.

Marsh, Ngaio. *A Man Lay Dead.* 1942

The guests at Sir Hubert's house party play a game of murder, but when someone takes the game too seriously, Inspector Roderick Alleyn must find the killer.

Mitchell, Gladys. *Speedy Death*. 1929

An explorer is murdered at Chayning Court, and Beatrice Adela Lestrange Bradley takes it upon herself to solve the crime.

Mortimer, John. *Rumpole of the Bailey*. 1978

Old barrister hack Horace Rumpole spends his time defending criminals in the courtrooms of the Old Bailey and defending himself from his wife at home.

Moyes, Patricia. *Dead Men Don't Ski*. 1960

While vacationing at an Italian ski resort with his wife, Inspector Henry Tibbett comes across evidence of smuggling and a murder.

Queen, Ellery. *The Roman Hat Mystery*. 1929

A lawyer is murdered while attending a play, and Ellery Queen learns almost everyone in the theater had a reason to kill him.

Sayers, Dorothy. *Whose Body*. 1923

An architect who finds a murdered man in his bathtub turns to Lord Peter Wimsey for help.

Stout, Rex. *Fer-de-Lance*. 1962

It takes Archie Godwin's legwork and Nero Wolfe's brains to explain the connection between the disappearance of an Italian immigrant and the death of a university president.

Taylor, Phoebe Atwood. *The Cape Cod Mystery*. 1931

Prudence Whitsby asks Asey Mayo, the "Codfish Sherlock," to look into things when her friend Bill Porter is charged with murdering a novelist.

Tey, Josphine. *The Franchise Affair*. 1949

A teenage schoolgirl who has been missing for weeks reappears and accuses two older women of holding her captive.

Wentworth, Patricia. *Grey Mask*. 1928

Charles Moray hires Miss Silver to discover if the woman who left him at the altar is involved in a kidnapping plot.

MYSTERIES FOR A BOOK DISCUSSION GROUP

Airth, Rennie. *River of Darkness.* 2000

Struggling to deal with the scars left from his experiences in World War I, Inspector John Madden returns to Scotland Yard only to be assigned a gruesome case that reminds him of the carnage of the recent war.

Burke, James Lee. *Purple Cane Road.* 2000

While working to clear the charges against a woman on death row, homicide investigator Dave Robicheaux searches for the person who murdered his mother thirty years ago.

Carr, Caleb. *The Alienist.* 1994

In turn-of-the-century New York City, a reporter and an "alienist," or psychologist, join forces with the police to stop a grisly killer who is targeting young transvestite prostitutes.

Cole, Jameson. *A Killing in Quail County.* 1996

In a small Oklahoma town in the 1950s, fifteen-year-old Mark Stoddard and his two friends try to find a bootlegger only to stumble onto a murder.

Cook, Thomas H. *The Chatham School Affair.* 1996

Henry Griswald remembers the day Miss Elizabeth Channing arrived in Chatham in 1926 to teach at the private boy's school only to be later accused of having an affair with another teacher and murdering her lover.

Crombie, Deborah. *Dreaming of the Bones.* 1997

Scotland Yard Superintendent Duncan Kincaid helps his ex-wife, Cambridge professor Victoria McClellan, when she becomes convinced that the subject of her new biography, poet Lydia Brooke, did not commit suicide but rather was murdered.

Edwards, Grace. *If I Should Die.* 1997

After stopping the attempted kidnapping of a classmate of her nephew, Mali Anderson comes across the body of the director of the Harlem Children's Choir lying in the street.

Fyfield, Frances. *A Question of Guilt.* 1988

London Crown Prosecutor Helen West and Detective Superintendent Geoffrey Bailey investigate the murder of a solicitor's wife who had something another woman wanted.

Gearino, G. D. *Blue Hole.* 1999

Kicked out of high school for defending a black football player in 1969, Charley Selkirk goes to work part-time for a local photographer and becomes involved in the search for a teenage boy who disappeared from a nearby hippie commune.

George, Elizabeth. *A Great Deliverance.* 1988

Urbane and charming Inspector Thomas Lynley and plain Sergeant Barbara Havers are sent to the wilds of Yorkshire to investigate a brutal murder.

Goddard, Robert. *Caught in the Light.* 1999

A married photographer has an affair with a mysterious woman in Vienna, but when he later tries to track her down, he learns he may be searching for a ghost.

Hambly, Barbara. *A Free Man of Color.* 1997

In antebellum New Orleans, where status and class are determined by a person's ancestry and skin color, Benjamin January, a free man of mixed blood, finds himself caught up in a murder that could have only happened in that city.

James, P. D. *Innocent Blood.* 1980

After turning eighteen, Philippa Palfrey goes searching for her birth parents and learns that her mother is just being released from prison.

Liss, David. *A Conspiracy of Paper.* 2000

Retired pugilist Benjamin Weaver sets aside his normal work of tracking down thieves in eighteenth-century London to investigate the death of his father, a stockjobber.

Maron, Margaret. *Bootlegger's Daughter.* 1992

While running for district judge, attorney Deborah Knott, the daughter of a retired bootlegger, is asked by Gayle Whitehead to find out who murdered her mom eighteen years ago.

McCrumb, Sharyn. *If Ever I Return, Pretty Peggy-O.* 1990

Peggy Muryan, a folksinger popular in the 1960s, moves back to the small Tennessee town where she grew up, seeking a means of reviving her career, but when she receives a threatening postcard, she turns to Sheriff Spencer Arrowood for help.

Parry, Owen. *Faded Coat of Blue.* 1999

In 1861 Washington, D.C., Welsh immigrant Captain Abel Jones is asked to investigate the murder of Anthony Fowler, a Union soldier and popular abolitionist.

Vine, Barbara. *Gallowglass.* 1990

A man recruits a young drifter who has recently been released from a mental institute to help him kidnap a woman with whom he has become obsessed.

Walker, Mary Willis. *Under the Beetles Cellar.* 1996

Lone Star Monthly magazine crime reporter Molly Cates is called in to assist the FBI, who are negotiating with religious fanatics holding a school-bus driver and eleven children hostage.

Walters, Minette. *The Ice House.* 1992

When a body is discovered in the old icehouse on the Grange, everyone wonders if it might not be Phoebe Maybury's husband, who disappeared ten years earlier.

ECCLESIASTICAL MYSTERIES

Black, Veronica. *A Vow of Silence.* 1990

Sister Joan finds it difficult to reconcile her interest in the mysterious events at the convent with her vow of obedience.

Blake, Michelle. *The Tentmaker.* 1999

Episcopalian priest Lily Connor wonders if the temporary post she is filling may have been vacated by murder.

Charles, Kate. *A Drink of Deadly Wine.* 1992

London solicitor David Middleton-Brown is called to probe the origins of a blackmail demand upon the priest of St. Anne's.

Chesterton, G. K. *The Innocence of Father Brown.* 1911

Father Brown, a shrewdly intuitive but unassuming priest, solves mysteries involving crime and human nature in this collection of short stories.

Frazer, Margaret. *The Novice's Tale.* 1992

Dame Frevisse, a fifteenth-century hosteler, intercedes when murder prevents a family from removing a novice from her convent.

Gallison, Kate. *Bury the Bishop.* 1995

Mother Lavinia Grey is at odds with her bishop—which makes her a suspect when he is murdered.

Gilman, Dorothy. *A Nun in the Closet.* 1975

Sisters John and Hyacinthe are improbable detectives when they sally forth to look over a mysterious property that has been willed to their convent.

Greeley, Andrew M. *Happy Are the Meek.* 1985

A classic "locked room" mystery with satanic overtones falls to Monsignor "Blackie" Ryan to investigate.

Greenwood, D. M. *Clerical Errors.* 1991

The severed head of the neighboring parish's pastor has Deaconess Theodora Braithwaite looking for clues among the men of the cloth.

Gur, Batya. *Murder on a Kibbutz.* 1994

When murder strikes the Jerusalem Psychoanalytic Institute, Chief Inspector Michael Ohayon suspects everyone at the institute.

Holland, Isabelle. *A Death at St. Anselm's.* 1984

The Reverend Claire Aldington appears to be the only person with a motive when St. Anselm's treasurer is murdered.

Holton, Leonard. *The Saint Maker.* 1959

Father Bredder discovers a severed head in the church, leading him to become a "policeman of God" in order to absolve falsely accused parishioners.

Joseph, Alison. *Sacred Hearts.* 1994

"Nun-at-large" Sister Agnes leaves the convent to help prove her ex-husband isn't a murderer.

Kemelman, Harry. *Friday the Rabbi Slept Late.* 1964

A young woman's murdered body is discovered in Rabbi David Small's car.

Kienzle, William X. *The Rosary Murders.* 1979

Father Koesler must solve a series of murders without breaking the sacred confidence of a murderer who confesses to his crimes.

Love, William F. *The Chartreuse Clue.* 1990

When a priest wakes up in the apartment of a murdered woman, Auxiliary Bishop Francis Regan takes the case.

Manuel, David. *A Matter of Roses.* 1999

Brother Bartholomew of Faith Abbey must solve a murder connected to his past.

McInerny, Ralph. *Her Death of Cold.* 1977

When a widow is found dead, locked into a freezer, Father Dowling joins the local police to determine the murderer.

O'Marie, Carol Anne. *A Novena for Murder.* 1984

Sister Mary Helen tries to find out whether Professor Villaneuva's death was caused by accident—or with malice aforethought.

Peters, Ellis. *A Morbid Taste for Bones.* 1977

Brother Cadfael encounters murder when he goes to Wales to obtain a saint's relics for his twelfth-century abbey.

Roe, Caroline. *Remedy for Treason.* 1998

Blind Jewish physician Isaac of Girona finds that the Black Death is not the only killer in his medieval Spanish town.

Smith, Charles Merrill. *Reverend Randollph and the Wages of Sin.* 1974

A female parishioner is found dead in the choir room of the Reverend Randollph's church.

Sullivan, Winona. *A Sudden Death at the Norfolk Café.* 1993

Sister Cecile can inherit a fortune only if she gives none of it to the church, so she sets up a private investigative business and donates the profits.

Telushkin, Joseph. *An Eye for an Eye.* 1991

When the father of a dead girl kills her murderer, Rabbi Winter defends his actions as illegal but perhaps not immoral.

Tremayne, Peter. *Absolution by Murder.* 1994

Sister Fidelma, both a medieval nun and an expert in the law of the time, is called to solve the murder of an abbess.

COZY MYSTERIES LIST

Abbott, Jeff. *Do unto Others.* 1994

After returning home to Mirabeau, Texas, to head the town's small library, Jordan Poteet finds himself accused of murdering a library censor.

Andrews, Donna. *Murder with Peacocks.* 1999

As a bridesmaid for three upcoming weddings, Meg Langslow has enough to do without trying to figure out who would want to kill the former sister-in-law of her soon-to-be-stepfather.

Atherton, Nancy. *Aunt Dimity's Death.* 1992

To claim a bequest in a will, American Lori Shepherd travels to England only to find that a fictional character from her childhood stories turns out to have been a real person.

Beaton, M. C. *Death of a Gossip.* 1985

Scottish Police Constable Hamish MacBeth is up to his hip waders in trouble when a local fly-fishing school hooks the body of a despised gossip columnist.

Borthwick, J. S. *The Case of the Hook-Billed Kites.* 1982

Sarah Dean, shepherding a gaggle of schoolgirls on an expedition to a Texas bird sanctuary, finds her proposed rendezvous with fellow teacher and boyfriend, Philip, is interrupted by murder.

Bowen, Rhys. *Evans Above.* 1997

Constable Evan Evans finds the peace of his village is shattered when two men die in the mountains of North Wales.

Brett, Simon. *A Nice Class of Corpse.* 1987

Mrs. Pargeter, a wealthy and engaging widow, realizes she must rely on her late husband's unusual legacy when she looks into the "accidental" death of an elderly woman staying at the same residential hotel.

Cannell, Dorothy. *The Thin Woman.* 1994

Overweight and overwrought interior designer Ellie Simons must lose sixty-three pounds if she wants to inherit her uncle's estate.

Carvic, Heron. *Picture Miss Seeton.* 1968

Spinster art teacher Miss Seeton discovers a real-life stabbing as she exits a performance of *Carmen*.

Churchill, Jill. *Grime and Punishment.* 1989

Jane Jeffrey, suburban mother and recent widow, finds herself playing sleuth in between PTA meetings and car-pool duties when a local cleaning woman is found strangled with her vacuum cleaner cord.

Dams, Jeanne M. *The Body in the Transept.* 1995

Tripping over a dead body in a cathedral transept is not the best way for expatriate American widow Dorothy Martin to spend her first Christmas in England.

Deloach, Nora. *Mama Stalks the Past.* 1997

Simone Covington helps her mama, Candi, figure out why a murdered woman who hardly spoke to Candi would leave her a substantial inheritance.

George, Anne. *Murder on a Girl's Night Out.* 1996

When big and brassy Mary Alice finds a man's body at the Skoot 'n' Boot, her country-western nightclub, she calls upon her little sister, Patricia Anne, to help solve the murder.

Harris, Charlaine. *Real Murders.* 1990

Aurora Teagarden, small-town librarian and member of a local club dedicated to the study of famous murders, suspects a club member when murders patterned after noteworthy killings start occurring.

Hart, Carolyn G. *Death on Demand.* 1987

Bookstore owner Annie Laurence snoops into the murder of a local mystery author who is killed during a weekly gathering of writers held at her store.

Holt, Hazel. *Mrs. Malory Investigates.* 1989

Middle-aged widow Sheila Malory promises to look after her friend Charlie's fiancée, but when the woman is found murdered, Mrs. Malory alleviates her guilt by investigating the crime.

Langton, Jane. *The Transcendental Murder.* 1964

Mary Morgan, a specialist in the New England Transcendentalists, finds Emerson scholar Homer Kelly extremely helpful when a murder occurs at the Patriot's Day celebration.

MacLeod, Charlotte. *Rest You Merry.* 1978

Professor Peter Shandy tries to outdo his neighbor's Christmas decorations with his own tacky display only to find someone has put a corpse in his living room.

Meier, Leslie. *Mail-Order Murder.* 1991

Working the night shift at a famous Maine mail-order company is murder when Lucy Stone discovers the body of the company's CEO in the parking lot.

Page, Katherine Hall. *The Body in the Belfry.* 1990

Minister's wife Faith Fairchild gets to know her neighbors when the body of a young, beautiful blackmailer is found in the church's belfry.

Shaber, Sarah R. *Simon Said.* 1997

Professor Simon Shaw of Kenan College is intrigued when the body of a murdered woman is unearthed in an archaeological excavation on the college grounds.

Sherwood, John. *Green Trigger Fingers.* 1985

Newly widowed Celia Grant's small horticultural business includes gardening on the side, but she didn't expect to find murder among the flower beds.

Skom, Edith. *The Mark Twain Murders.* 1989

When a student suspected of plagiarism is found dead in the university library, Professor Beth Austin hunts for the killer with the help of an FBI agent.

Trocheck, Kathy Hogan. *Every Crooked Nanny.* 1992

Callahan Garrity, former Atlanta cop and current owner of a house-cleaning service, investigates the disappearance of a nanny.

Wolzien, Valerie. *Murder at the PTA Luncheon.* 1987

The murder of two PTA members pushes suburban Connecticut housewife and PTA vice president Susan Henshaw to search for the killer.

CULINARY CRIMES

Bishop, Claudia. *A Taste for Murder.* 1994

As owners of the Hemlock Falls Inn, sisters Sarah and Meg feel compelled to investigate when one of their guests is discovered dead at the annual Hemlock Falls History Days festival.

Bond, Michael. *Monsieur Pamplemousse.* 1985

Retired from the Surete, gastronome Monsieur Pamplemousse and his faithful dog Pommes Frites find his new job as a food critic nearly as demanding when a man's severed head is served as the specialty of the day.

Childs, Laura. *Death by Darjeeling.* 2001

Indigo Tea Shop owner Theodosia Browning plays amateur detective when a guest is found murdered at a historic homes garden party she catered.

Davidson, Diane Mott. *Catering to Nobody.* 1990

When her ex-father-in-law is nearly poisoned at an affair she catered, Goldy Bear decides to do some sleuthing before the police close her business permanently.

Fairbanks, Nancy. *Crime Brûlée.* 2001

Culinary writer Carolyn Blue goes looking for a missing friend who may have become an appetizer for alligators.

Farmer, Jerrilyn. *Sympathy for the Devil.* 1998

After Hollywood producer Bruno Huntley is found dead at a star-studded party that she catered, Madeline Bean must find the real killer if she wants to keep her partner out of jail.

Fluke, Joanne. *Chocolate Chip Cookie Murder.* 2000

When the Cozy Cow Dairy's deliveryman is found murdered behind her bakery, Hannah Swensen, owner of The Cookie Jar, finds she not only has a talent for baking cookies, but also for solving crimes.

King, Peter. *The Gourmet Detective.* 1996

Specializing in locating rare and obscure ingredients, the Gourmet Detective is asked by Scotland Yard to assist when a journalist is murdered at the prestigious Circle of Careme banquet.

Lamalle, Cecile. *Appetite for Murder.* 1999

Charles Poisson, chef at La Fermette, upstate New York's finest temple of gastronomy, finds a nasty surprise in his mushroom patch: the body of a woman.

Laurence, Janet. *A Deepe Coffyn*. 1989

When a food critic is killed with a boning knife at a historical cooking symposium, chef Darina Lisle decides not to stew among the suspects, but to solve the case.

Lyons, Nan, and Ivan Lyons. *Someone Is Killing the Great Chefs of Europe*. 1976

It takes a pastry chef and a fast-food entrepreneur to crack the case when the world's most famous chefs are murdered in the manner of their own culinary specialties.

Myers, Amy. *Murder at the Smokehouse*. 1997

While visiting the Tabor family for a gala ball in 1901, chef and sometime-sleuth August Didier and his wife, Tatiana, stumble upon a corpse in Lady Tabor's smokehouse.

Myers, Tamar. *No Use Dying over Spilled Milk*. 1997

Pennsylvania Dutch inn owner Magdalena Yoder finds that her cousin is really and truly lactose intolerant when his body is discovered in a tank of milk.

Pence, Joanne. *Something's Cooking*. 1993

Sassy food columnist Angelina Amalfi finds life is a banquet until a man who has contributed recipes to her column is found dead.

Rich, Virginia. *The Cooking School Murders*. 1982

Returning to Harrington, Iowa, for her annual visit, Mrs. Genia Potter takes an advanced cooking class for fun, but she discovers a murderer has enrolled along with her.

Richman, Phyllis. *The Butter Did It*. 1997

Restaurant critic Chas Wheatley suspects that the death of superstar chef Laurence Levain is caused by more than just his high cholesterol level, and he sets out to prove it.

Russell, Charlotte Murray. *Cook Up a Crime.* 1951

"Full-fashioned" spinster Jane Amanda Edwards needs Jesse Nye's family recipes for her cookbook, but when Jesse winds up dead, Jane begins searching for a killer with a recipe for murder.

CULTURALLY
DIVERSE DETECTIVES

Native American

Cole, David. *Butterfly Lost.* 1999

Even though Hopi Laura Winslow's business is finding people, she is reluctant to take the case of a young girl who is missing from the reservation.

Doss, James D. *The Shaman Sings.* 1994

The omens that appear to Ute shaman Daisy Perika help Police Chief Scott Parris find the solution to the murder of a science graduate student.

Hager, Jean. *The Grandfather Medicine.* 1989

Police Chief Mitch Bushyhead's Cherokee background isn't necessarily a help in a murder case that appears to have ties to a secret Cherokee society.

Jones, Stan. *White Sky, Black Ice.* 1999

Alaskan trooper Nathan Active, an Inupiat raised by white adoptive parents, finds himself culturally conflicted as he investigates a pair of seeming suicides.

Lane, Christopher A. *Season of Death.* 1999

Inupiat police officer Ray Attla is disconcerted to pull in a human head on the end of his fishing line.

Perry, Thomas. *Vanishing Act.* 1995

Seneca Jane Whitefield's unusual business of helping people disappear is threatened when a client may not be what he seems.

Stabenow, Dana. *A Cold Day for Murder.* 1992

Ex-D.A. Kate Shugak has returned to her roots in the Alaskan bush, but she comes out of retirement to search for a missing park ranger and the guide who went looking for him.

Afro-American

Carter, Charlotte. *Rhode Island Red.* 1997

Nanette Hayes has an advanced degree but prefers to make her living playing the saxophone on New York streets—until an undercover cop is killed in her apartment.

Greer, Robert O. *The Devil's Hatband.* 1996

C. J. Floyd, Denver bail bondsman and bounty hunter, is hired to find a young girl and recover some important documents from a band of environmental extremists.

Grimes, Terris McMahon. *Somebody Else's Child.* 1996

A murder and kidnapping in her mother's deteriorating Sacramento neighborhood prompt a reluctant Theresa Galloway to investigate.

Himes, Chester. *The Crazy Kill.* 1959

Harlem policemen "Grave Digger" Jones and Ed "Coffin" Johnson look into a stabbing at a wake that seems connected to a robbery.

Mosely, Walter. *Devil in a Blue Dress.* 1990

Easy Rawlins doesn't really consider himself a detective, but he's broke enough to take a missing person case.

Neely, Barbara. *Blanche on the Lam.* 1992

Blanche's past as a passer of bad checks leads her to take a domestic position in a southern house filled with conflict—and murder?

Sallis, James. *Long-Legged Fly.* 1992

A period of several years covers four episodes of cases for New Orleans P.I. Lew Griffin.

West, Chassie. *Sunrise.* 1994

> D.C. cop Leigh Anne Warren figures a visit to her small hometown will help her recover from the stress of a difficult case, and she's right, until murder intervenes.

Latino

Burns, Rex. *The Alvarez Journal.* 1975

> Denver police detective Gabriel Wager's case involves an import shop suspected of being a front for marijuana smugglers.

Cook, Bruce. *Mexican Standoff.* 1988

> Antonio "Chico" Cervantes, Los Angeles private eye, stumbles into the international drug trade when the search for a hit-and-run driver takes him to Mexico.

Corpi, Lucha. *Eulogy for a Brown Angel.* 1992

> Gloria Damasco's extrasensory perception keeps returning to an incident when she discovered the dead body of a child.

Garcia-Aguilera, Carolina. *Bloody Waters.* 1996

> Cuban American P.I. Lupe Solano accepts a case involving an adopted child with a rare genetic disease.

Ramos, Manuel. *The Ballad of Rocky Ruiz.* 1993

> An incident of Chicano activism in the 1970s leads to ex-activist Luis Montez's involvement in murder in the 1990s.

Asian American

Brown, Mark. *Game Face.* 1991

> Ex-detective Ben McMillen returns to the Kona, Hawaii, police force when his former partner's wife is assaulted and murdered.

Cunningham, E. V. *The Case of the Angry Actress.* 1967

> Beverly Hills detective Masao Masuto discovers the death of a movie mogul is only one in a series of murders.

Furutani, Dale. *Death in Little Tokyo.* 1996

Ken Tanaka pretends to be a private investigator only to be startled when Rita Newly comes to him with a case of blackmail.

Massey, Sujata. *The Salaryman's Wife.* 1998

Rei Shimura, a Japanese American making a living by teaching English in Japan, becomes involved in the murder of a businessman's wife.

Wingate, Anne. *Death by Deception.* 1988

FBI Agent Mark Shigata is suspended from the agency when he is the prime suspect in the murder of a woman whose body is found in his own backyard.

FICTION NOIR AND NEO-NOIR

Anderson, Edward. *Thieves Like Us.* 1937

A small band of desperate men succeed in breaking out of jail only to go back to the work they know: robbing banks.

Cain, James M. *Double Indemnity.* 1936

A small-time, small-souled insurance agent plots with a bored house-wife to kill her husband.

Caspary, Vera. *Laura.* 1942

Policeman Mark McPherson finds himself falling in love with a dead woman—the victim of the crime he is investigating.

Colbert, James. *Profit and Sheen.* 1986

A cocaine dealer and a violent ex-cop combine forces to make a big deal.

Ellroy, James. *L.A. Confidential.* 1990

Three cops in 1950s Los Angeles, one sad and flawed, the other two downright crooked, find themselves inextricably entwined in crime.

Fischer, Bruno. *The Evil Days.* 1973

When Caleb Dawson's wife claims that she "found" a fortune in jewelry, it begins a downward spiral in their lives.

Goodis, David. *The Moon in the Gutter*. 1953

A romance between a Philadelphia stevedore and a fashionable society girl is colored by his obsession with his sister's death.

Gresham, William Lindsay. *Nightmare Alley*. 1946

A glib carnival hustler and his fortune-telling wife are con artists who make a killing—in every sense of the word.

Hendricks, Vicki. *Miami Purity*. 1995

Ex-stripper Sherise takes a job at a dry-cleaning shop as a first step in bettering herself but then sets her sights on the owner's son.

Hughes, Dorothy. *Ride the Pink Horse*. 1946

A Chicago gangster arrives in Santa Fe during fiesta time with blackmail as his intent.

Marlowe, Dan J. *The Name of the Game Is Death*. 1962

When a bank robbery goes wrong, a double cross between partners in crime is only to be expected.

Matheson, Richard. *Now You See It*. 1994

A once great magician, now living on the charity of his son, who has succeeded him, discovers a murderous plot.

McCoy, Horace. *They Shoot Horses, Don't They?* 1935

Two disaffected drifters meet and decide to participate in a dance marathon that leads to violence and murder.

Pelecanos, George P. *Shame the Devil*. 2000

Murderous mayhem follows when two vicious brothers attempt to rob a restaurant.

Phillips, Clyde. *Fall from Grace*. 1998

David Perry's drunken confession concerning his wealthy but erring wife to a stranger leads to murder.

Phillips, Scott. *The Ice Harvest*. 2000

It may literally be a cold day in hell when lawyer-turned-mobster

Charlie Anglist and fellow bad guy Vic are able to leave town with the money they have embezzled.

Pronzini, Bill. *Blue Lonesome.* 1995

Lonely Jim Messenger is compelled to discover the secrets behind the beautiful woman he sees at the Harmony Café.

Reed, Philip. *Bird Dog.* 1997

A beautiful woman convinces former car salesman Harold Dodge to help her when a used-car dealer cheats her.

Ridley, John. *Stray Dogs.* 1997

John Stewart is stuck in a burg that's the next thing to a ghost town—and he's willing to make a few ghosts get out.

Ring, Ray. *Arizona Kiss.* 1991

Cynical journalist Mackey becomes involved with his tipster, a beautiful woman who convinces him to help her swindle a local judge.

Thompson, Jim. *The Killer Inside Me.* 1952

A folksy, slow-talking sheriff in a tiny Texas town is a secret serial murderer.

Whittington, Harry. *Web of Murder.* 1958

Lawyer Charles Browers has fallen in love with his beautiful secretary, Laura, and wants to lose his wife but keep her money.

Willeford, Charles. *Pick-Up.* 1955

Beautiful, amoral alcoholic Helen meets starving artist–waiter Harry; did she pick him up, or was it the other way around?

Woodrell, Daniel. *Give Us a Kiss.* 1996

Doyle tried to escape his white-trash past, but when he heads home to the Ozarks, he becomes entangled in his infamous brother's legal problems and a family blood feud.

Woolrich, Cornell. *The Bride Wore Black.* 1940

When Julie becomes first a bride, then a widow, she is determined to avenge her husband's death.

ANIMAL-LOVERS MYSTERIES

Adamson, Lydia. *A Cat in the Manger*. 1990

Unemployed actress and cat-lover Alice Nestleton enjoys her cat-sitting jobs, but she didn't expect to find the body of her employer amongst his purebred Himalayan cats.

Allen, Garrison. *Desert Cat*. 1994

Mystery bookstore owner Penelope Warren and her Abyssinian cat Big Mike find small-town life in the Southwest can be murder!

Banks, Carolyn. *Death by Dressage*. 1993

Fellow horseback rider Veronica's technique had been as dreadful as her personality, but when she dies as a result of being kicked by a horse, Robin Vaughn suspects foul play.

Benjamin, Carol Lea. *This Dog for Hire*. 1996

It's only appropriate that Rachel Alexander, dog trainer turned private eye, and her partner, a pit bull named Dashiell, take the case of a missing basenji and a murdered artist.

Berenson, Laurien. *A Pedigree to Die For*. 1995

When Melanie's Uncle Max, breeder of championship standard poodles, is found dead on the kennel floor and a prizewinning stud turns up missing, her Aunt Peg persuades her to do some undercover sleuthing.

Braun, Lilian. *The Cat Who Could Read Backwards*. 1966

Journalist Jim Qwilleran doesn't realize that when he finds the body of snobby art columnist George Mountclemons, spunky Siamese cat Koko is the one actually uncovering the clues.

Brown, Rita Mae. *Wish You Were Here*. 1990

Tiger cat Mrs. Murphy and her sidekick, Welsh corgi Tee Tucker, follow the scent when their owner, postmistress Mary Minor "Harry" Harristeen, realizes that seemingly pleasant postcards are actually death threats.

Conant, Susan. *A New Leash on Death*. 1990

An obedience class ends in murder, and *Dog Life* columnist Holly Winter finds Rowdy, the "orphaned" Malamute dog, a great help in digging up clues.

Douglas, Carole Nelson. *Catnap*. 1992

Feline private eye Midnight Louie discovers a murdered man on the floor of a Las Vegas conference and selects publicist Temple Barr as his human assistant in solving the case.

Gordon, Mildred, and Gordon Gordon. *Undercover Cat*. 1963

The FBI puts D. C., the undercover cat, under surveillance when he returns home from a night prowl with the wristwatch of a kidnapped woman around his neck.

Jaffe, Jody. *Horse of a Different Killer*. 1995

Horse-loving reporter Natalie Gold investigates when an expensive show horse and a top trainer are found dead side by side.

Lanier, Virginia. *Death in Bloodhound Red*. 1995

Jo Beth Sidden, breeder and trainer of bloodhounds used for search-and-rescue missions, smells trouble when she is suspected of murder.

Moore, Barbara. *The Doberman Wore Black*. 1983

Veterinarian Gordon Christy first sees the Doberman at the site of a near accident and later acquires the dog when its owner is found dead.

Murphy, Shirley Rousseau. *Cat on the Edge*. 1996

An accident gives tomcat Joe Grey the ability to understand, read, and speak human speech, so he turns his feline talents to private investigation and undertakes a case of murder.

O'Kane, Leslie. *Play Dead*. 1998

Dog therapist Allie Babcock uses her insight and skills when she suspects her canine client's owner was murdered.

Wilson, Karen Ann. *Eight Dogs Flying*. 1994

Veterinary technician Samantha Holt assists Louis Agustin, D.V.M., in more than just giving shots when she tries to find out why local greyhounds are suddenly becoming vicious.

GAY AND LESBIAN MYSTERIES

Aldyne, Nathan. *Vermilion*. 1980

Bartender Dan Valentine and his straight friend and business associate find location is everything when they open a bar across from a police station in Boston's South End.

Baker, Nikki. *In the Game*. 1991

Black stockbroker Virginia Kelly's best friend from business school, Bev, asks for her help when Bev's partner is found dead.

Baxt, George. *A Queer Kind of Death*. 1966

Black, gay New York police detective Pharaoh Love looks into the case of a murdered actor-model.

Beecham, Rose. *Introducing Amanda Valentine*. 1992

Ex-N.Y.P.D., now a police detective inspector in New Zealand, Amanda Valentine must find the vicious killer the press has dubbed the "Garbage Dump Killer."

Calloway, Kate. *First Impressions*. 1996

Cassidy James is brand new to the P.I. business, but even she knows it's not a good idea to fall in love with a woman accused of murder.

Craft, Michael. *Flight Dreams*. 1997

Reporter Mark Manning's publisher gives him an unusual assignment: prove that an heiress, missing for seven years, is alive.

Cutler, Stan. *Best Performance by a Patsy*. 1991

Aging P.I. Rayford Goodman wants gay ghostwriter Mark Bradley to write his life story, but when he is waylaid and beaten up on his way to meet Mark, it's apparent that someone is afraid of what Goodman may reveal.

Fennelly, Tony. *The Glory Hole Murders.* 1985

Matt Sinclair, former New Orleans D.A. who now owns a furniture store, finds himself involved in the case of a man found murdered in the men's room of a gay bar.

Forrest, Katherine V. *Amateur City.* 1984

L.A.P.D. detective Kate Delafield investigates a case of murder in a high-rise office whose residents were united in their dislike of the murdered man.

Hart, Ellen. *Hallowed Murder.* 1989

Jane Lawless and her friend Cordelia Thorn become sleuths when a University of Minnesota sorority sister is found dead.

Hunter, Fred. *Government Gay.* 1997

Alex Reynolds and his partner, Peter, are completely at a loss when Alex is accused of possessing secret government information.

Maddison, Lauren. *Deceptions.* 1999

Mystery novelist Connor Hawthorne finds life imitates art when her lover is killed and she becomes determined to find her killer.

Maiman, Jaye. *I Left My Heart.* 1991

Formerly a travel writer and a novelist and now a private eye, Robin Miller goes to San Francisco to investigate the death of a former lover.

Maney, Mabel. *The Case of the Not-So-Nice Nurse.* 1993

Comparisons are inevitable when Cherry Aimless seeks the help of intrepid gal detective Nancy Clue in this funny parody of the popular Nancy Drew series.

McDermid, Val. *Report for Murder.* 1987

Scottish journalist Lindsay Gordon's friend is a suspect in the murder of a famous cellist.

McNab, Claire. *Lessons in Murder.* 1988

Australian Detective Inspector Carol Ashton finds her investigation into a schoolteacher's murder is complicated by her attraction to the prime suspect.

Michaels, Grant. *A Body to Die For.* 1990

Boston hairdresser Stan Kraychik is not the outdoorsy type, but when a park ranger he has a crush on dies, Stan is determined to brave Yosemite Park and flush out the killer.

Nava, Michael. *The Little Death.* 1986

Self-described "fag lawyer" Henry Rios feels compelled to look into the suspicious death of a former friend and lover.

Raphael, Lev. *Let's Get Criminal.* 1996

Professor Nick Hoffman fears that his partner, Stefan, may have killed the English department's newest hire.

Scoppettone, Sandra. *Everything You Have Is Mine.* 1991

When a victim of rape becomes a murder victim, New York private eye Lauren Laurano is determined to find the person responsible.

Stevenson, Richard P. *Death Trick.* 1981

Gay P.I. Donald Strachey and his lover, Timothy Callahan, find themselves enmeshed in dirty politics in Albany, New York.

Wilson, Barbara. *Gaudi Afternoon.* 1990

Free-spirit Spanish translator Cassandra Reilly takes on the job of locating a missing person in Barcelona.

Wilson, John Morgan. *Simple Justice.* 1996

Reporter Benjamin Justice, still mourning his dead lover and trying to outlive a newspaper scandal, is recruited by his former boss to look into a killing associated with a gay bar.

Zimmerman, R. D. *Closet.* 1995

TV news reporter Todd Mills is involuntarily outed when the man who was his secret lover is murdered.

Zubro, Mark. *A Simple Suburban Murder.* 1990

Chicago high school teacher Scott Carpenter and his lover, pro base-ball player Scott Carpenter, try their hands at detection when Scott's fellow teacher is murdered.

C

Genre Resources

For reference resources, we've compiled annotated lists of print and electronic resources that we have found helpful and interesting. Every effort has been made to include information that is accurate and current as of June 2001. However, because of the ephemeral nature of publishing, especially on the Internet, we cannot guarantee the availability of all the resources listed. We hope we've given a generous number, which may compensate for any resources that may no longer be available or even exist. And, of course, you'll want to add to our lists any ones you like and find useful.

MYSTERY GENRE PERIODICALS

Alfred Hitchcock's Mystery Magazine. ISSN 0002-5224. P.O. Box 54011, Boulder, CO 80322-4011. 800-333-3311, ext. 4000. $33.97 per year. Published monthly except for a July/August double issue.

Short stories by some of today's top mystery writers. Also includes one mystery classic short story and a mystery book review column.

Deadly Pleasures. ISSN 1069-6601. P.O. Box 969, Bountiful, UT 84011-0969. $14 per year. Published quarterly. http://www.deadly pleasures.com.

Excellent resource that includes interviews with mystery authors, reviews of current mystery fiction, articles on collecting mysteries, and other topics. Unique features include the periodical's "reviewed to death" section, in which one mystery title is reviewed by several different people.

The Drood Review of Mystery. ISSN 0893-0252. 484 East Carmel Drive, no. 378, Carmel, IN 46032. $17 per year. Published bimonthly. http://www.droodreview.com.

A mix of in-depth and short reviews of mystery fiction as well as the occasional author interview or article. Includes a semiannual preview of forthcoming mystery books.

Ellery Queen's Mystery Magazine. ISSN 0012-6328. P.O. Box 54052, Boulder, CO 80322-4052. 800-333-3053. $33.97 per year. Published monthly except for a combined September/October issue.

Mystery short stories by a wide range of authors. Includes a book review column by distinguished mystery critic Jon L. Breen.

Murder Most Cozy. Jan Dean. P.O. Box 561153, Orlando, FL 32856. 407-481-9481. $15 per year. Published bimonthly. E-mail: jandean@bellsouth.net.

Our favorite mystery newsletter has everything the cozy lover needs and wants. Includes interviews with cozy mystery authors, short descriptions of new cozy mysteries, and a section dedicated to "crimeless cozies."

Mystery News. ISSN 734-9076. Black Raven Press. PMB 152. 262 Hawthorne Village Commons, Vernon Hills, IL 60061. Fax: 847-680-0346. $20 per year. Published bimonthly. http://www.blackraven press.com.

If you can only afford one mystery review source for your library, this is the one to get. A terrific mix of author interviews and in-depth reviews of current mystery fiction. Each issue includes a preview section of forthcoming titles as well as information on mystery awards, conferences, and more.

Mystery Readers Journal: The Journal of Mystery Readers International. ISSN 1043-3473. MRI. P.O. Box 8116, Berkeley, CA 94707. 510-845-3600. $24 per year for membership in Mystery Readers International. Published quarterly. http://www.mysteryreaders.org.

Each issue focuses on a particular theme such as mysteries set in France, religious mysteries, or academic mysteries. Articles written about this theme, articles by authors who write that type of mystery, and book reviews of selected mysteries are included. Each issue also offers a section devoted to awards and mystery happenings.

The Mystery Review. ISSN 1192-8700. C. von Hessert and Associates, Ltd. The Mystery Review. P.O. Box 488, Wellesley Island, NY 13640-0488. 613-475-4440. Fax: 613-475-3400. $20 per year. Published quarterly. E-mail: mysterv@reach.net. http://www.inline-online/mystery/.

Includes interviews with authors and lengthy articles on different mystery topics. Includes a selective number of book reviews and a section dedicated to new releases.

MYSTERY REFERENCE SOURCE BOOKS

Derie, Kate, ed. *The Deadly Directory.* 2001

This source will interest mystery writers as well as readers, as it includes mystery booksellers, publishers of mystery novels and magazines that accept mystery short stories, and even publications relating to mysteries. Other items include up-to-date lists of author newsletters, websites, and e-mail addresses.

Heising, Willetta L. *Detecting Men: A Reader's Guide and Checklist for Mystery Series Written by Men.* 1998

A compendium of male mystery authors who are still alive and writing, this source is a great one for answering the question, "Which title comes first in this series?" and features a number of appendixes listing characters, mysteries by locations, and more.

Heising, Willetta L. *Detecting Women: A Reader's Guide and Checklist for Mystery Series Written by Women.* 3d ed. 2000

Similar to the compendium above but listing female mystery authors who are still alive and writing.

Herald, Diana Tixier. *Genreflecting: A Guide to Reading Interests in Genre Fiction.* 5th ed. 2000

Many different types of genres, including romance, adventure, westerns, and crime fiction, are given in this detailed listing of genre fiction.

The chapter on crime fiction includes dozens of different types and themes and offers interesting lists, including one of fictional detective biographies, anthologies, bibliographies, mystery associations and conventions, and even book clubs.

Herbert, Rosemary. *The Oxford Companion to Crime and Mystery Writing.* 1999

An alphabetical listing of articles on the history of crime and mystery writing, seminal authors, canons, subgenres, and more.

Huang, Jim, ed. *100 Favorite Mysteries of the Century: Selected by the Independent Mystery Booksellers Association.* 2000

Here, independent mystery booksellers share their knowledge, tastes, and choices for the best mystery novels of the century, including lists arranged both chronologically and alphabetically by author with book descriptions. The listing of independent mystery bookstores is also of interest.

Hubin, Allen J. *Crime Fiction II: A Comprehensive Bibliography, 1749–1990.* 1994

Using a broad definition of crime fiction, the author covers all such fiction published in book format in English. Provides detailed author bibliographies with indexes by setting, series, title, and author. The update to this book was published in CD-ROM format and is available from Locus Press.

Husband, Janet G., and Jonathan F. Husband. *Sequels: An Annotated Guide to Novels in Series.* 3d ed. 1997

A source that offers, in many cases, annotated lists of genre sequels, including many mystery series. A great help in all kinds of readers' advisory. Title and subject indexes are included.

King, Nina, with Robin Winks. *Crimes of the Scene.* 1997

A reader's guide for the international traveler, this features mysteries set around the world.

Lachman, Marvin. *The American Regional Mystery.* 2000

A useful, if not comprehensive, listing of mystery authors and novels by the regions in the United States they feature. Perfect for use in creating displays of regional mysteries.

Miller, Ron. *Mystery! A Celebration.* 1996

The rumored demise of the much-loved *Mystery!* television series on PBS makes this compendium of the program's famous shows even more appealing. This features loads of photos from the various programs and lots of information on everything from the hosts to the actors to the mystery writers. Not just fun to browse, this can serve as an excellent resource when it comes to selecting videos and DVDs for your library.

Nichols, Victoria, and Susan Thompson. *Silk Stalkings: More Women Write of Murder.* 1998

A compendium created by lovers of the genre specifically to compile mystery fiction books by female writers, this source is divided into subgenres, such as "Senior Sleuths," and includes appendixes giving series character chronologies and author pseudonyms. A useful source for readers' advisory.

Panek, LeRoy Lad. *An Introduction to the Detective Story.* 1987

A scholarly, yet accessible, discussion of the history of the detective story.

Pederson, Jay P., and Taryn Benbow-Pfalzgraf, eds. *The St. James Guide to Crime and Mystery Authors.* 4th ed. 1996

One in the St. James Guide to Writers series (formerly known as the Twentieth-Century Writers series), this guide includes short biographies and articles discussing English-language authors of crime, mystery, and thriller fiction. A plus is the listing of all publications by each author, including plays, screenplays, and so forth.

Penzler, Otto. *101 Greatest Films of Mystery and Suspense.* 2000

Compiled by the knowledgeable Penzler (owner of the famous Mysterious Bookshop in New York), this list comes complete with cast lists, behind-the-scenes gossip, and plot twists. A good resource for those choosing DVDs or videos for a popular collection, this is also just plain fun to read.

Penzler, Otto, and Mickey Friedman. *The Crown Crime Companion: The Top 100 Mystery Novels of All Time.* 1995

The members of the Mystery Writers of America selected their favorite mystery novels, and Friedman and Penzler compiled and annotated the list in this entertaining, slim volume. Also included are essays by such well-known mystery authors as H. R. F. Keating and Mary Higgins Clark.

Saricks, Joyce G. *The Readers' Advisory Guide to Genre Fiction.* 2001

Adventure, mystery, suspense, and thrillers are four of the fifteen fiction genres covered in this outstanding introduction to genre fiction. Those readers' advisors unfamiliar with mystery fiction and its many permutations will find this to be a good starting point in learning more about these genres and their appeal to readers.

Stine, Kate, ed. *The Armchair Detective Book of Lists: A Complete Guide to the Best Mystery, Crime, and Suspense Fiction.* 2d ed., rev. 1995

A source useful to mystery readers and collectors, this gives a complete listing of all the mystery and suspense awards, lists of fan clubs and collectors' and writers' organizations, obscure lists such as the most frequently taught crime and mystery writers, and even some lists of personal favorites by authors such as Aaron Elkins and Tony Hillerman.

Swanson, Jean, and Dean James. *By a Woman's Hand: A Guide to Mystery Fiction by Women.* 2d ed. 1996

This source, which focuses on women mystery writers, includes biographical profiles and offers read-alikes—useful suggestions along the lines of "if you like E. X. Giroux's novels featuring British barrister Robert Forsythe, you might also enjoy Sara Woods's novels featuring barrister Antony Maitland." Indexes include lists of series characters, geographic settings, and detective type of profession. Some changes have been made since the first edition, published in 1994, so libraries will want to keep the first edition to refer to.

Swanson, Jean, and Dean James. *Killer Books: A Reader's Guide to Exploring the Popular World of Mystery and Suspense.* 1998

An enjoyable guide listing several subgenres, including romantic suspense, and giving suggestions for further reading and films of interest.

What Do I Read Next? A Reader's Guide to Current Genre Fiction. Current

This reference source is now published twice a year as well as available as a Web-based product. The mystery section is provided by mystery critics, publishers, and booksellers Tom Schantz and Enid Schantz and should be required reading for all mystery readers' advisors. Each mystery entry includes basic bibliographic details as well as information on where reviews of the mystery appeared and even offers read-alikes.

Winks, Robin W., and Maureen Corrigan, eds. *Mystery and Suspense Writers: The Literature of Crime, Detection, and Espionage.* 1998

This two-volume set, part of the Scribner Writers Series, gives biographies of authors, discussions of plots and characters, and selected bibliographies, written by leading authors and specialists in the field of mystery and detective fiction. A listing of themes and subgenres, including armchair detectives and gay and lesbian mystery fiction, is included.

INTERNET SITES

The African American Mystery Page   http://www.aamystery.com

A source of information on African American mystery authors, new releases, contribution to the literature by ethnic authors, and so forth.

The American Crime Writers League   http://www.ACWL.org

This site, created by a group of mystery writers, contains capsule reviews, interviews, conference information, author tour schedules, and more.

The Archive of Mystery and Suspense Fiction
http://www.hycyber.com/MYST

This site contains links to mystery and suspense fiction writers, directories that include lists of fictional characters in mysteries, author pseudonyms, award-winning books and authors, and film and fiction archival information.

Black Bird Mysteries   http://www.blackbird-mysteries.com

An online mystery bookstore offering recommended reading suggestions for all kinds of mystery and suspense fiction as well as true crime books. Information on book series, mystery websites, and award lists can also be found.

Book Wire   http://www.bookwire.com

You'll find book industry news, features, reviews, guides to literary events, author interviews, and thousands of annotated links to book-related websites here.

BookBrowser: The Guide for Avid Readers
http://www.bookbrowser.com

This provides links to mystery fiction subgenres, including historical, animal, and humorous mysteries.

Clue Lass   http://www.cluelass.com

A continuous forecast of more than 100 new mystery books, listings of independent booksellers, mystery-related websites, mystery book award nominees, and more.

The Crime Writers Association   http://www.thecwa.co.uk

This website for the British association offers highlights from their newsletter, lists of events, award nominees and winners, and more.

The Crime Writers of Canada   http://www.crimewriterscanada.com

Here you'll find information on Canadian mystery authors, portions of the association newsletter, lists of Arthur Ellis Award winners, and even bookstores that are CWC members.

DorothyL—The Official Website
http://www.kovacs.com/DOROTHY/dorothyl.htm

This unique discussion group offers information and discussion of assorted mysterious topics posted by lovers of the genre.

Genrefluent—The World of Genre Fiction   http://www.genrefluent.com

Created by Diana Tixier Herald, the author of the valuable print resource *Genreflecting: A Guide to Reading Interests in Genre*

Fiction, this site provides links to all kinds of mystery fiction as well as numerous library links, an author index, and handouts for workshops.

The Gumshoe Site   http://www.nsknet.or.jp/~jkimura

This lists award winners, new and forthcoming mystery titles, and author and conference news and information.

The Historical Mystery Appreciation Society
http://www.members.home.net/monkshould/hmas-index

Featuring information on the "history mystery," this site offers articles, research and writing tips, book reviews, and news on upcoming historical mystery fiction.

The Independent Mystery Booksellers Association
http://www.mysterybooksellers.com

This home page for the IMBA offers titles for suggested reading, information about booksellers, Dilys Award nominees and winners, favorite mysteries of the century, and bookseller data.

Lady M's Mystery International   http://www.mysteryinternational.com

Lady M offers mystery book reviews, interviews with authors, original mystery fiction, lists of favorite titles, and much more.

The Mysterious Home Page
http://www.webfic.com/mysthome/mysthome.htm

A generously annotated and comprehensive guide to mystery resources on the Internet, this includes newsletters; information about conferences, conventions and seminars, organizations, and awards; and even games.

Mysterious Strands
http://www.idsonline.com/userweb/cwilson/mystery.htm

This offers information on authors, mystery reference sources, readers' and writers' conferences, awards, bookstores, and publishers.

The Mystery Writers of America   http://www.mysterywriters.net

The website of the MWA, this site offers Edgar Award nominees and winners lists and information on conferences and membership.

MysteryNet: The Online Mystery Network   http://www.mysterynet.com

This site contains reviews of mystery fiction, readers' advisory suggestions, profiles of mystery authors, and information on awards, events, and organizations of interest to lovers of the genre.

Partners and Crime Mystery Booksellers   http://www.crimepays.com

Here you'll find information on mystery author readings and signings, links to author websites, author interviews, and recommended readings.

The Poisoned Pen   http://www.poisonedpen.com

This website is also an online newsletter for this mystery bookstore and provides information on upcoming events, author visits, recommended readings, and reviews.

St. Martin's Minotaur   http://www.minotaurbooks.com

This offers suggested reading for all types of mystery genres and includes links to mystery author websites. The entertaining online newsletter *Murder at the Flatiron* is located on this website.

Sisters in Crime   http://www.sistersincrime.org

Details on joining Sisters in Crime, a list of their members' books in print, links to author member websites, local chapters of Sisters in Crime, and upcoming events are all included on this organization's website.

Tangled Web UK   http://www.twbooks.co.uk

A British site that reviews crime, mystery, and fantastic fiction books and features profiles of more than 300 authors as well as information, mystery news, views, and events.

Tart City   http://www.tartcity.com

This humorous website specializes in crime fiction featuring independent-minded female sleuths.

The Thrilling Detective   http://www.thrillingdetective.com

A hard-boiled noir website offering author information, new and forthcoming books, videos and movies, award information, and mystery fiction links.

Select Bibliography

Bailey, Frankie Y. 1991. *Out of the Woodpile: Black Characters in Crime and Detective Fiction.* Westport, Conn.: Greenwood.

Baker, Robert A., and Michael T. Nietzel. 1985. *Private Eyes: 101 Knights: A Survey of American Detective Fiction, 1922–1984.* Bowling Green, Ohio: Bowling Green State Univ. Popular Press.

Balcom, Ted, ed. 1997. *Serving Readers.* Fort Atkinson, Wis.: Highsmith.

Ball, John, ed. 1976. *The Mystery Story.* San Diego: Univ. of California.

Barron, Neil, Daniel S. Burt, Melissa Hudak, D. R. Meredith, Mary Pat Radke, Kristin Ramsdell, Tom Schantz, and Enid Schantz, eds. Vol. 2. 2000. *What Do I Read Next? A Reader's Guide to Current Genre Fiction.* Detroit: Gale.

Beinhart, Larry. 1996. *How to Write a Mystery.* New York: Ballantine.

Bendel, Stephanie. 1983. *Making Crime Pay: A Practical Guide to Mystery Writing.* New York: Prentice-Hall.

Blades, John. 1995. True Fact or Wanton Fiction? *Chicago Tribune,* October 15.

Block, Lawrence. 1993. A Modest Proposal for the Categorization of Mysteries. In *The Fine Art of Murder: The Mystery Reader's Indispensable Companion,* edited by Ed Gorman, Martin H. Greenberg, Larry Segriff, with Jon L. Breen. New York: Carroll & Graf.

Block, Lawrence. 1979. *Writing the Novel from Plot to Print.* Cincinnati: Writer's Digest Books.

Blythe, Hal. 1993. *Private Eyes: A Writer's Guide to Private Investigating.* Cincinnati: Writer's Digest Books.

Breen, Jon L. 1998. The Legal Crime Novel. In *Mystery and Suspense Writers: The Literature of Crime, Detection, and Espionage.* New York: Scribner.

Broderick, Dorothy M. 1993. How to Write a Fiction Annotation. *VOYA* 15, no. 6 (February): 333.

Buchanan, Sally A. 1994. The Ties that Bind: Library Binding. *Wilson Library Bulletin* 68, no. 6 (February): 52–53.

Carr, Robyn. 1992. *Practical Tips for Writing Popular Fiction.* Cincinnati: Writer's Digest Books.

Chandler, Raymond. 1944. The Simple Art of Murder. *Atlantic Monthly* (December): 53–59.

Clute, John, and John Grant, eds. 1997. *The Encyclopedia of Fantasy.* New York: St. Martin's.

Collingwood, Donna, ed. 1993. *Mystery Writer's Marketplace and Sourcebook.* Cincinnati: Writer's Digest Books.

Coonts, Stephen. 1990. Revealing the Secrets of the Technothriller. *Writer's Digest* (August): 18–21.

Cox, Michael, ed. 1997. *The Oxford Book of Spy Stories.* Oxford: Oxford Univ. Press.

Dahlin, Robert. 1996. Expanding the Scene of the Crime. *Publishers Weekly* (April 22): 38–47.

Dove, George N., and Earl F. Bargainnier, eds. 1986. *Cops and Constables: American and British Fictional Policemen.* Bowling Green, Ohio: Bowling Green State Univ. Popular Press.

Dreyer, Eileen. 1997. Elements of Romantic Suspense. In *Writing Romances: A Handbook by the Romance Writers of America.* Cincinnati: Writer's Digest Books.

Garson, Helen S. 1996. *Tom Clancy: A Critical Companion.* Westport, Conn.: Greenwood.

Gerard, Philip. 1996. *Creative Nonfiction: Researching and Crafting Stories of Real Life.* Cincinnati: F & W Publications.

Gorman, Ed, Lee Server, and Martin H. Greenberg, eds. 1998. *The Big Book of Noir.* New York: Carroll & Graf.

Gorman, Ed, Martin H. Greenberg, Larry Segriff, with Jon L. Breen, eds. 1993. *The Fine Art of Murder: The Mystery Reader's Indispensable Companion.* New York: Carroll & Graf.

Grafton, Sue, ed. 1992. *Writing Mysteries: A Handbook by the Mystery Writers of America.* Cincinnati: Writer's Digest Books.

Grape, Jan, Dean James, and Ellen Nehr, eds. 1998. *Deadly Women: The Woman Mystery Reader's Indispensable Companion.* New York: Carroll & Graf.

Heising, Willetta L. 1998. *Detecting Men: A Reader's Guide and Checklist for Mystery Series Written by Men.* Dearborn, Mich.: Purple Moon.

Heising, Willetta L. 2000. *Detecting Women: A Reader's Guide and Checklist for Mystery Series Written by Women.* 3d ed. Dearborn, Mich.: Purple Moon.

Herald, Diana Tixier. 1999. *Fluent in Fantasy: A Guide to Reading Interests.* Englewood, Colo.: Libraries Unlimited.

Herald, Diana Tixier. 2000. *Genreflecting: A Guide to Reading Interests in Genre Fiction.* 5th ed. Englewood, Colo.: Libraries Unlimited.

Herbert, Rosemary, ed. 1999. *The Oxford Companion to Crime and Mystery Writing.* New York: Oxford Univ. Press.

Hoffert, Barbara. 1998. Book Report: What Public Libraries Buy and How Much They Spend. *Library Journal* 123, no. 3 (February 15): 106–10.

Huang, Jim. 2000. *100 Favorite Mysteries of the Century: Selected by the Independent Mystery Booksellers Association.* Carmel, Ind.: Crum Creek Press.

Hubin, Allen J. 1994. *Crime Fiction II: A Comprehensive Bibliography, 1749–1990.* New York: Garland.

Husband, Janet G., and Jonathan F. Husband. 1997. *Sequels: An Annotated Guide to Novels in Series.* 3d ed. Chicago: American Library Association.

Jacob, Merle. 2001. Weeding the Fiction Collection; or, Should I Dump *Peyton Place? Reference and User Services Quarterly* 40, no. 3 (spring): 234–39.

Jacobsohn, Rachel W. 1994. *The Reading Group Handbook: Everything You Need to Know, from Choosing Members to Leading Discussions.* New York: Hyperion.

Jones, Patrick. 1998. *Connecting Young Adults and Libraries.* 2d ed. New York: Neal-Schuman.

Jute, Andre. 1987. *Writing a Thriller.* New York: St. Martin's.

Keating, H. R. F. 1991. *Writing Crime Fiction.* New York: St. Martin's.

King, Nina, with Robin Winks. 1997. *Crimes of the Scene: A Mystery Novel Guide for the International Traveler.* New York: St. Martin's.

Kinnell, Margaret, ed. 1991. *Managing Fiction in Libraries.* London: Library Association Publishing.

Klein, Kathleen Gregory, ed. 1994. *Great Women Mystery Writers: Classic to Contemporary.* Westport, Conn.: Greenwood.

Lachman, Marvin. 2000. *The American Regional Mystery.* Minneapolis: Crossover.

Laskin, David, and Holly Hughes. 1995. *The Reading Group Book: The Complete Guide to Starting and Sustaining a Reading Group, with Annotated Lists of 250 Titles for Provocative Discussion.* New York: Plume.

Malice Domestic One: An Anthology of Original Traditional Mystery Stories. 1992. New York: Pocket Books.

Malling, Susan, and Barbara Peters, eds. 1998. *AZ Murder Goes Classic: Current Crimewriters Revisit Past Masters.* Scottsdale, Ariz.: Poisoned Pen.

Maryles, Daisy. 2001. It's Grisham Time. *Publishers Weekly* (January 8): 22.

McCook, Kathleen de la Pena, and Gary O. Rolstad, eds. 1993. *Developing Readers' Advisory Services: Concepts and Commitments.* New York: Neal-Schuman.

McCormick, Donald, and Katy Fletcher. 1990. *Spy Fiction: A Connoisseur's Guide.* New York: Facts on File.

Miller, Ron. 1996. *Mystery! A Celebration: Stalking Public Television's Greatest Sleuths.* San Francisco: Bay Books and Tapes.

Moody, Susan, ed. 1990. *Hatchards Crime Companion: The Top 100 Crime Novels Selected by the Crime Writer's Association.* London: Hatchards.

Murphy, Bruce F. 1999. *The Encyclopedia of Murder and Mystery.* New York: St. Martin's Minotaur.

Mystery Writers of America. 1995. *The Crown Crime Companion: The Top 100 Mystery Novels of All Time*. New York: Crown.

Newton, Michael. 1989. *How to Write Action-Adventure Novels*. Cincinnati: Writer's Digest Books.

Nichols, Victoria, and Susan Thompson. 1998. *Silk Stalkings: More Women Write of Murder*. Lanham, Md.: Scarecrow.

Norville, Barbara. 1986. *Writing the Modern Mystery*. Cincinnati: Writer's Digest Books.

O'Brien, Geoffrey. 1997. *Hardboiled America: Lurid Paperbacks and the Masters of Noir*. Exp. ed. New York: Da Capo.

Ocork, Shannon. 1989. *How to Write Mysteries*. Cincinnati: Writer's Digest Books.

Ousby, Ian. 1997. *Guilty Parties: A Mystery Lover's Companion*. New York: Thames and Hudson.

Palmer, Jerry. 1979. *Thrillers: Genesis and Structure of a Popular Genre*. New York: St. Martin's.

Panek, Leroy Lad. 1987. *An Introduction to the Detective Story*. Bowling Green, Ohio: Bowling Green State Univ. Popular Press.

Pearsall, Jay. 1995. *Mystery and Crime: The New York Public Library Book of Answers—Intriguing and Entertaining Questions and Answers about the Who's Who and What's What of Whodunnits*. New York: Simon and Schuster.

Pederson, Jay P., and Taryn Benbow-Pfalzgraf, eds. 1996. *St. James Guide to Crime and Mystery Writers*. 4th ed. Detroit: St. James.

Pelzer, Linda C. 1995. *Mary Higgins Clark: A Critical Companion*. Westport, Conn.: Greenwood.

Penzler, Otto. 2000. *101 Greatest Films of Mystery and Suspense*. New York: Simon and Schuster.

Penzler, Otto, and Mickey Friedman. 1995. *The Crown Crime Companion: The Top 100 Mystery Novels of All Time*. New York: Crown.

Pringle, Mary Beth. 1997. *John Grisham: A Critical Companion*. Westport, Conn.: Greenwood.

Pronzini, Bill, and Marcia Muller. 1986. *1,001 Midnights: The Aficionado's Guide to Mystery and Detective Fiction*. New York: Arbor House.

Provost, Gary. 1991. *How to Write and Sell True Crime.* Cincinnati: Writer's Digest Books.

Ramsdell, Kristin. 1999. *Romance Fiction: A Guide to the Genre.* Englewood, Colo.: Libraries Unlimited.

Rees Cheney, Theodore A. 1991. *Writing Creative Nonfiction: How to Use Fiction Techniques to Make Your Nonfiction More Interesting.* Berkeley, Calif.: Ten Speed.

Roberts, Gillian. 1999. *You Can Write a Mystery.* Cincinnati: Writer's Digest Books.

Rochman, Hazel. 1987. *Tales of Love and Terror: Booktalking the Classics, Old and New.* Chicago: American Library Association.

Romance Writers of America. *Romance Novels—Industry Statistics* [Home Page of the Romance Writers of America], [Online]. Available at http://www.rwanational.com/statistics.stm. [August 28, 2001].

Ross, Catherine Sheldrick, and Mary K. Chelton. 2001. Reader's Advisory: Matching Mood and Material. *Library Journal* 126, no. 2 (February 1): 52–55.

Rule, Ann. 1991. Why I Write about Murder. *Good Housekeeping* (September): 42–48.

Ryan, Valerie. 1991. Ann Rule: Psychopathic Killers Are Her Specialty in the True-Crime Genre. *Publishers Weekly* (May 3): 54–55.

Saricks, Joyce G. 2001. *The Readers' Advisory Guide to Genre Fiction.* Chicago: American Library Association.

Saricks, Joyce G., and Nancy Brown. 1997. *Readers' Advisory Service in the Public Library.* 2d ed. Chicago: American Library Association.

Sauer, Patrick. 2000. *The Complete Idiot's Guide to Starting a Reading Group.* Indianapolis, Ind.: Alpha Books.

Senkevitch, Judith J., and James H. Sweetland. 1994. Evaluating Adult Fiction in the Smaller Public Library. *RQ* 34, no. 1 (fall): 78–89.

Senkevitch, Judith J., and James H. Sweetland. 1996. Evaluating Public Library Adult Fiction: Can We Define a Core Collection? *RQ* 36, no. 1 (fall): 103–17.

Skillman, T. Macdonald. 2000. *Writing the Thriller.* Cincinnati: Writer's Digest Books.

Slezak, Ellen. 1995. *The Book Group Book: A Thoughtful Guide to Forming and Enjoying a Stimulating Book Discussion Group.* 2d ed. Chicago: Chicago Review Press.

Slote, Stanley J. 1997. *Weeding Library Collections: Library Weeding Methods.* 4th ed. Englewood, Colo.: Libraries Unlimited.

Smith, Myron J., Jr., and Terry White. 1995. *Cloak and Dagger Fiction: An Annotated Guide to Spy Thrillers.* 3d ed. Westport, Conn.: Greenwood.

Stine, Kate, ed. 1995. *The Armchair Detective Book of Lists: A Complete Guide to the Best Mystery, Crime, and Suspense Fiction.* 2d ed. New York: Otto Penzler Books.

Swanson, Jean, and Dean James. 1996. *By a Woman's Hand: A Guide to Mystery Fiction by Women.* 2d ed. New York: Berkley.

Swanson, Jean, and Dean James. 1998. *Killer Books: A Reader's Guide to Exploring the Popular World of Mystery and Suspense.* New York: Berkley.

Symons, Julian. 1993. *Bloody Murder: From Detective Story to the Crime Novel.* 3d ed. New York: Mysterious.

Winks, Robin W., and Maureen Corrigan, eds. 1998. *Mystery and Suspense Writers: The Literature of Crime, Detection, and Espionage.* New York: Scribner.

Winn, Dilys. 1984. *Murder Ink: Revived, Revised, Still Unrepentant.* New York: Workman Publishing.

Woods, Paula L., ed. 1995. *Spooks, Spies, and Private Eyes: Black Mystery, Crime, and Suspense Fiction of the Twentieth Century.* New York: Doubleday.

Wortman, William A. 1989. *Collection Management: Background and Principles.* Chicago: American Library Association.

Yaakov, Juliette, and John Greenfieldt, eds. 2001. *Fiction Catalog.* 14th ed. New York: Wilson.

INDEX

Authors, editors, titles, subjects, and series
are interfiled in one alphabet. Authors print
in roman, titles in italics, subjects in
boldface, and series in quotation marks.

John Charles is a reference librarian and fiction selector for the Scottsdale Public Library system. A reviewer for *Booklist* and *Library Journal,* John has coauthored articles on collection development and genre fiction. He and Joanna Morrison write *Voice of Youth Advocates'* annual "Clueless: Adult Mysteries with Young Adult Appeal" list.

Joanna Morrison is a reference librarian and nonfiction selector for the Scottsdale Public Library system. She gives booktalks to groups and has presented several programs on booktalking for Arizona Library Association conferences. In addition to contributing mystery reviews to *Voice of Youth Advocates,* she joins John Charles in an annual article for *VOYA* on the year's best adult mysteries for young adults.

Candace Clark has worked for the Scottsdale Public Library system since 1975 and has served as a youth librarian since 1986. She is heavily involved in material selection, youth programming, and booktalking for all ages. Clark was chair of the Children's Services' Roundtable for the Arizona Library Association and has presented many programs on booktalking for librarians. Since 1991, she has cohosted *Booktalk,* a city cable monthly book review and author interview program in Scottsdale.